Endorsements

We all have a story and a journey where we work out who we are and in particular who God is for us. And, how we can know Him and walk in His ways.

No one's story would fit neatly into a made for TV format where the happy ending falls tidily between the last set of commercials and the program credits. Stories are messy affairs and journeys have an up and down quality to them that might make a seasoned sailor seasick! If our stories are to be authentic then they cannot be homogenous. The glory of God's love is seen in the mess we create and the beauty of His own good nature as He pursues us with His loving-kindness.

Carol's story is not for the fainthearted, nor is it for the plastic Christian who is easily offended by chaos, confusion and human turmoil.

For us to be consistent in God's love we must encounter Him in all of our personal disarray. Our predicaments never put God off from being the epitome of our loving attention. His affection and passion for us shines through our story making it into an epic of grace and mercy.

Carol is a brave woman who has endured much. Her writing reveals her courage, backlit by the incredible passion that God has for her personally. She has prevailed in awful circumstances because the Lord never let go of her and she learned to cling on to His love and goodness.

I recommend this book to you wholeheartedly. I hope you find yourself on her journey. Like Carol, I hope you rewrite the story of your life in the beauty of how God sees you. A wise person would use this book as a catalyst for his or her own upgrade.

Graham Cooke
Author, speaker
www.brilliantbookhouse.com
www.brilliantperspectives.com

"There's nothing more encouraging to me than when someone is willing to share the story of their journey of brokenness to discovering grace. Carol writes with a ruthless and raw honesty combined with a sincere faith in Christ that will give hope to the broken heart."

Derek Levendusky,
Author, worship leader,
Lead pastor of GraceLife Church
www.dereklevendusky.com.

I love how God brings people into my life. There are no coincidences with God so I must assume that meeting Carol DuPre' was no accident. I didn't know her while she was going through some of her darkest times. I've only begun to know her as she's come out the other end, having traveled through a twisted and hazardous tunnel and into the light of Jesus. Carol's story is a testimony to the healing love of God, who comforts us and soothes us and helps us grow. She makes herself totally vulnerable and at the same time there's a bit of mischief in her that inspires a laugh or two! Come along side her and see how the Lord has restored her heart and soul. You'll come to love her as I do.

Ethel M. Chadwick
Host of Bagels and Blessings Radio Show
Rochester, NY
www.bagelsandblessings.com

When does expressing your truest self, created in God, become rebellion? When does questioning the standards of a community become borderline insanity? When does being the scapegoat for the guilt of others become acceptable?

When control and legalistic adherence to the rules, for the sake of Christ, of course, define your Christian experience. Carol DuPre', in her authentically raw, and often witty book, "Broken," blows the whistle on a form of Christianity that she bought hook, line, and sinker, one which would cause years of profound grief and pain.

But as graphic as the gory details are, even more, Carol lifts us up to a higher plane as she paints a gloriously beautiful picture of Love Himself, hearing her cry and coming to her aid. In her journey to truth and wholeness, Carol makes a startling discovery.... the approval she desperately sought through the traditions of men, was already hers in the arms of her God. This is a poignant and immensely significant book for any sincere Christian to read.

Maryann Ehmann, author, speaker, spiritual and business coach and mentor.
MaryannEhmann.com;
haveievertoldyou.com

There is a Redeemer. Carol DuPre' has indeed carried a pregnancy to full term and brought forth life in the delivery of her words here. In the process, the Consummate Midwife, The Spirit of God, has birthed Carol with the truth of who she is in her inward parts.

I have known Carol for many years. I am absolutely verklempt * at what Papa God has done, what He is doing, and what He shall yet do.

Carol's journey into wholeness is a catalyst. Her bravery will reap the rewards of freedom for others.

As the song says, "...You're not broken anymore, you're not captive anymore. I love you. Mercy is yours...." (Aaron Keyes, "Not Guilty Anymore." See p. 318.)

Christine O'Riley, RN
(Obstetrics and Women's Health)
Loved daughter of Papa God
Friend of Carol DuPre'

* "Verklempt" is a Yiddish word meaning being so impacted by something that takes your breath away that you cannot even speak to describe it. Often it refers to being emotionally overwhelmed in a very good way...such as ... when we experience something amazing beyond words.

Broken

a pastor's wife shares her story

Carol DuPré

OlivePress
צהר זית

Published by

Olive Press צהר זית
Messianic and Christian Publisher

www.olivepresspublisher.com

Messianic & Christian Publisher

Our prayer at Olive Press is that we may help make the Word of Adonai fully known, that it spread rapidly and be glorified everywhere. We hope our books help open people's eyes so they will turn from darkness to Light and from the power of the adversary to God and to trust in ישוע Yeshua (Jesus). (From II Thess. 3:1; Col. 1:25; Acts 26:18,15 NRSV and CJB, the *Complete Jewish Bible*) May this book in particular help bring Yeshua's bruised and battered sheep back into His fold.

In honor to God, pronouns referring to the Trinity are capitalized, satan's names are not. But not all Bible versions do this and legally must be printed as they are.

Cover art © 2013 by Marty Yokawonis
   http://marty12cats.wix.com/mtyokawonis
   Her Etsy store: http://www.etsy.com/shop/PaintersLoft
Title font called "a bite" © 2013 by Billy Argel,
   http://billyargelfonts.blogspot.com/
Interior design by Olive Press

BROKEN A Pastor's Wife Tells Her Story

ISBN 978-0-9855241-8-0
Printed in the USA.
1. Christian Inspirational 2. Christian Personal Growth 3. Personal Memoirs

All Scriptures unless otherwise marked are taken from the NEW KING JAMES VERSION of the Bible. Copyright © 1982 by Thomas Nelson, Inc. All rights reserved.

Scriptures marked:

NASB are taken from the NEW AMERICAN STANDARD BIBLE®, Copyright © 19 60,1962,1963,1968,1971,1972,1973,1975,1977,1995 by The Lockman Foundation. Used by permission

NRSV are taken from the NEW REVISED STANDARD VERSION of the Bible, copyright © 1989 National Council of the Churches of Christ in the USA. Used by permission. All rights reserved.

KJV are taken from the KING JAMES VERSION of the Bible.

"A woman's strength isn't just how much she can handle before she breaks. It's also about how much she can handle after she's broken."

From Facebook, author unknown

TABLE OF CONTENTS

(Cont.)

TABLE OF CONTENTS (Cont.)

Prologue

There is no way this story could be told until now. Until now, the hurt, confusion, anger and complete lack of mercy would have gushed from every word. It would have hit you square in the eye and all you would have seen is what I lacked, how much growing I still needed to do, and very little of what He has done for my soul.

If certain couples waited for their relationship to be perfectly in order before they married, they might not marry at all. If they waited for their finances to flourish before they had a child, they might remain childless. If I wait until I am totally healed and healthy in my head before I tell my story, the story would never be told because part of my healing may come with the telling, and my very need for healing is also part of the story. None of us have arrived.

Walking with Christ is a process. Like any relationship, there are a number of "things" that have to be worked out. The fact that any head butting that happens is with my head alone and He never moves His is what makes this walk such a challenge.

"I am the Lord, I change not," is His response to my whiny, *"Work with me on this, will You?"*

It is all about the grace factor. Our shortcomings will show up as sure as the sun will set tonight. What we do about facing them determines the direction we take and the transformation we make.

He's all about change. I'm all about Him.

It makes for a good start and a better finish.

INTRODUCTION

Where To Start

A memoir that sits in your head and never makes it to paper, or nowadays, the web, doesn't automatically become a book. It is, as they say, an idea waiting to happen; but as long as it only simmers in the mind, it remains dead in the water. No one will know what has really taken place in your life. People desire the tangible, legible, hold-in-your-hand, touch-it truth. Or else they will just imagine what really happened and it might actually be far from reality.

I admit it—I'm struggling to take the words soaring in my head and connect them to paper. The process allows all the awful times to come to life again. I'm forced to section it together in bite-size pieces. And, if I use my words to bring life to a sad story, will it again give life to the sadness in my own heart and keep my healing at bay?

Too much in one day and all that darkness comes back and I have to mentally and emotionally start my recovery from scratch. I've already written chapter after chapter about what happened and how I reacted to it and how the Lord stuck it out with me and where I am today with the experience, yet a lot of it still doesn't make sense because I'm still waiting for the ending.

You'll get it when I've got it.

Of one simple thing I am sure:

He told me to tell you my story.

He told me to make sure He was mentioned in every chapter. He didn't need to be named or given a title or a reference point because the readers would know He was there.

And then He said He'll take care of the rest of it—and me, junk included.

I know I'm just putting a book together, but it all sounds eerily familiar to the Christian walk, doesn't it?

This desire to tell you about what happened wars with this voice in my head that says I'm gossiping. I haven't yet arrived at a place where my heart and my mind are in sync and utterly pure. Isn't that supposed to be the criteria for sharing? I fear some of that negativity might spill out into the language and the story-telling experience will reek with bitterness and bad attitude. Therefore, I assume I must wait until I get *there*.

But I may never get *there* and this might *never* get written.

It's sort of like cleaning the house before the maid arrives, or "cleaning up your act" before you ask Jesus to come into your heart. I'm trying to clean myself up first, in order to have the right to tell you what happened.

Or does the fact that it *happened* to me **give** me the right to tell it?

My intentions are good but they are also sometimes religious, and that's exactly what I'm trying to get away from. When you've been immersed in legalism, you think like that. It's that double-minded man thingy.

These are the kinds of things I struggle with, the thoughts I carry, forgetting that it's really all about Him.

Will I ever arrive?

Maybe not. Maybe the war that ensues is part of the plan. Maybe that's what we are all about—a people on the go who never really get *there*, but spend our whole life trying.

I'll start by asking the question no really mature Christian person is supposed to ask:

"Why me?"

These things just don't happen to ordinary people. But we're extraordinary people, remember? A peculiar people. We've made a word like *peculiar* into *weird, strange, abnormal* when it's really more like *uncharacteristic, astonishing, unique.*

When we make a decision to follow after Jesus, the rest of the decisions after that aren't necessarily our own. Nor are they necessarily fully embraced. But, ah yes, they ARE peculiar.

In my case, they were never embraced at all. I'm still not sure if I have ever put my arms around anything that's happened to me over the last few years, the years that have elapsed since the Awakening (**my** title), but the Lord knows I've tried. When you have been broken for years, in one form or another, you find it hard to embrace anything but your sanity.

Oh, yeah, and He took that, too. Chapter 7.

Don't you dare read ahead.

What happened to me in my story, sitting at the point-of-impact in a church split, a wretched divorce, and a 21st century excommunication, is comparable to a bus crashing through a guardrail and hurtling down a steep embankment. We were all in this together, we were all sitting in different places on the bus and we all succumbed to varying degrees of injury. In my vignettes, I often refer to the experience as a bus crash.

These vignettes were written at various times along this journey; they are not necessarily chronological or theme-connected, which is why there is a timeline included at the end of the book. They were birthed out of unusual and sometimes grueling periods of depression and confusion. The better ones sprang forth out of victory transcending from an awareness of a heavenly Father caring immensely for His daughter. Each vignette tells its own story and while some of the themes and messages may overlap in the telling, they all point to a bigger theme and a much bigger story.

It is a story I am compelled to tell you for the simple reason that someone has to tell it. So many tales in church get shoved under the carpet. Lumpy carpets can lead to casualties if you're not careful. To make the walk a lot less treacherous, I'm going to rip up that carpeting and reveal some of what's been hidden underneath.

Hello

The light on my phone machine was blinking on and off. Someone named Private Caller had left a message. I was about to be slammed.

The caller told me that everything bad that happened to me was because "God doesn't sleep," that He knows what's going on and everything wrong I ever did or said in my life was coming back to me and offering me the miserable life I deserved.

She concluded the call by telling me that I was the "rottenest person in the whole world," and she hoped I would go on to lead a lonely and empty life.

For the most part, from where I was at emotionally at the time, she was dead-on right.

Broken

The guest speaker was a charismatic man from the Vineyard Ministries. It took a lot of persuasion to bring him to our church because our pastor was, among other things, in disagreement with their casual style of dress. One of the elders convinced our pastor that the man might be safe, reminding him that this man was originally from this general area and didn't get back home very often and so he agreed to let the speaker lead one of the week-end church services.

I knew the man personally and I knew he was safe.

He began by introducing himself through his testimony and his connection to the area and somewhere in the middle of describing himself, made the simple statement that he came from a "broken home."

He did? I never realized that about the man. How sad.

Until I remembered that the man was my younger brother.

I had never used that phrase before—*broken home*—and it alarmed me to see myself that way: that I, too, had come from that same "broken home." Our parents had been divorced for decades and I was trying my best not to look at the situation in terms of brokenness, because that might imply that something in my past was irreparable or that maybe I, too, was broken. And that my brokenness, in many ways, may have contributed to my own broken-down marriage with the pastor who did not agree with the Vineyard style of dress, the one who nervously allowed his brother-in-law to steal the pulpit for just this one small service, the one who would soon divorce me for *Cruel and Inhumane Treatment* because he couldn't sue me for abandonment or adultery.

The one who was **really** broken himself.

Like me.

Like all of us.

Stark Naked

The pastor's wife is naked wherever she goes. She lives in a glass house with glass closets, glass bedrooms and glass bathrooms. Every wandering eye follows her as she goes about living a life that is no different than anyone else's except that she is expected to be more perfect, which isn't even a possibility. You can't be more than perfect without crossing the line, once again, into imperfection.

I once read that a pastor's wife is scrutinized far more than the pastor. If she's okay, then she's being treated right. I wasn't okay and I didn't know why.

The wife of the pastor is often expected to *perform* in a certain way. Performing is acting. I didn't like to pretend; I yearned to be real.

She is asked to *conform* a lot. I didn't like the idea of having to imitate someone else or conform to someone else's expectation; I yearned to be myself.

None of these things help a pastor's wife, or anyone else for that matter, towards *transformation*, which is what is supposed to happen if we are, indeed, in Christ. Transformation is the wonderful side product of hanging out with the King.

I made a decision to hang out with the King, but it required walking away from what and who I knew. It demanded I finally be real and it began to expose someone I missed and hadn't recognized in a long time. The real me.

Recently, Father told me I wasn't naked any more. I began to understand that I was only transforming for an audience of one. I was fully clothed and I didn't have to fake a thing or cover up unattractive body parts. I could be myself and if there was anything that needed transforming, and of course there was, He would kindly point it out and we would deal with it—in His way and in His timing.

I looked forward to that because I missed being me.

It's taking us a long time to find all of me, but I'm definitely in there and I am definitely coming out. The real me might have been one of those lumps shoved under the carpet.

Except for authors mentioned, the only real names used in this book are in the Joy, Grace, and Sharon stories.

Section One

"The thief does not come except to steal and to kill and to destroy..." John 10:10

Chapter One

MY YOUNG LIFE

Family

My father was a POW from World War II and unlike many of his fellow veterans, told his version of the story over and over to anyone who would listen. That included me, his firstborn and only daughter, who grew up believing Dad had to be some kind of war hero. He never told me, or anyone else for that matter, that his own father had already battered and bruised him long before that fateful day his plane was shot down over Germany. The prison camp held him for four long months, but it was the timing that saved him—1945—and he returned home to marry my Mom faster than you can say "Post-Traumatic-Stress-Disorder."

Dad never knew how to vent all the pain mounting inside of him, so he took it out on the kids he fathered and unfortunately, I became his first whipping post.

My parents were very young when they married and when I was just two years old, my father went to live with a friend and my mother went to live with her sister. It marked the beginning of multiple separations that led, years later, to divorce. That first time they broke up, my parents left me for two years with my sixty-year-old grandmother who did her best to make me feel wanted.

Still, and it is my only memory of this age, I would climb onto the sofa in the living room, peer out the front window and cry for my daddy and mommy to come home.

My grandmother's son, a slightly disturbed young man, lived there, too, and he also did his best to make me feel wanted.

He turned the dark and crowded attic of his mother's house into his private sanctuary. He decorated his walls and ceiling with hand-drawn sketches that displayed a genuine gift only shared with occasional visitors. I have to admit I never knew why he wanted to live there when there were other bedrooms to choose from. He lived a strictly regimented lifestyle that included daily morning bus rides downtown, afternoons spent reading incessantly, washing the dinner dishes, and fondling as many of his nieces as occasion allowed. He was intelligent, attractive, artistic, and perverted, and the family managed to cover up the perverted part until some forty years later when the cousins started talking. I was now no longer alone with the knowledge of my uncle's secret, but it didn't make me feel any better and it was already too late.

He had drawn my picture in pencil on the sloped ceiling of that nook—just above the bed he slept in—and every night, my face was the last face he saw.

I also saw his face every night.

****

The small Catholic Church stood across the street from the rectory. I couldn't remember it ever being full except on Christmas Eve, when it always smelled, just slightly, of Manhattans. I would go to the rectory every Sunday after Mass and count the offering, earning money to pay for a week's worth of treats at the local teen hang-out. The parish priest always made some sort of physical connection with me every week that began with innocent and gentle touches and culminated in sloppy, wet kisses. He was more than four times my age. What happened in that nicely furnished parlor never made its way to the surface of my thoughts until years later, when Catholic priests and all their dirty, little deeds were the headlines of every newspaper in America. I had only wanted extra money to buy a coke and a donut.

By then, I was already haunted by past recollections that made no sense, a history of migraines, irrational fears, and frequent memory loss exacerbated by anything with confrontational overtones. A CT-scan didn't reveal an abnormal mass in or on my brain or my body and prescription drugs were unable to pull it out by the roots.

It all mingled in with my Daddy's whippings and my uncle's touches and I'm convinced that for decades I wore an invisible sandwich sign over my neck that said, "ABUSE ME."

Because they did.

I'm still kneeling on my couch, looking out the window and waiting for Daddy to come back and hold me and promise me he won't leave me ever again.

This is exactly how we come into the Kingdom—broken and bruised and in desperate need of healing and holding.

We've been looking for you, Daddy, all our lives.

Fire Places

"If Jesus wants to save me He can come down off his high throne in heaven and do it Himself!"

Those words, and the normal telephone good-byes, were the last ones I heard my uncle say to me. Two weeks later, they found him dead from a massive heart attack. He was alone in his own bedroom, face down in his own feces, making it easy for my cousin to find him.

I was just a little girl. I think I was too small to understand and too scared to tell anyone and too trusting to believe that what was happening was anything but normal. I was lying on my Uncle's bed and staring at the ceiling and we were talking and he said to me,

"So whose face do you see up there?"

I saw that it was my face.

My uncle had drawn it himself, in pencil, and it looked exactly like me because he was a good artist. His slanted bedroom ceiling, up there in my grandmother's attic, was his personal Sistine Chapel project and I guess that made me a work of art. I was, after all, his favorite niece. Actually, I thought it a waste of a gift that this man, who could draw so well, would use his bedroom ceiling to display this picture of my face and those of two of my cousins, who also visited him up there.

In his will, I inherited a small portion of the money he managed to save by living with his mother and drawing unemployment. I bought myself a gas fireplace.

History With Dad

PTSD * is something they never knew or understood after World War II. It was my own generation, and the war in Vietnam, that opened our eyes to its horrific symptoms. I had my own form of it, having served in the atmosphere of war that waged in my home—its source in the heart of my father's rage. The sound of a car door closing sometime around 4:30 PM threw me emotionally to the floor as I anticipated the release of that pent-up fury in the form of a hard smack to the back of my head.

His favorite element, it seemed, was that of surprise. He would sneak up behind me, and suddenly I would feel that sting coming from the knuckle of his right hand pointer-finger and I would jump. I would always jump. And I knew my punishment was over, at least for whatever it was I did wrong while he was at school teaching. I walked on egg-shells until bedtime.

He was a high school teacher and he was a good one. He loved history, and he loved his students, and he loved it when they came to love history, too. It was my worst subject. I hated it.

Doesn't take a psychoanalyst to figure that one out.

Apparently, and according to my mother, daily whacks were a reoccurring theme in our house. Like a bad habit, you just get used to it because that's what people do and this is your life. I had nothing else to compare it to, so I emotionally labeled it as normal behavior and expected it. Until the one day it exploded.

33

Dad and I were standing outside, in the country, with no one around, next to the foundation of a house we were building. We had lived in as many apartments and houses as my numerical age (I was in my early teens) and this would be the first home we ever owned. I have no idea what we were talking about except that I must have said something he didn't like. All I remember is being thrown to the ground and kicked repeatedly until I thought I would die because I couldn't breathe without pain. I have no idea what Dad said after that point or whatever it is that finally made him stop. My memory only recalls what the end of his shoe felt like and the terror that came with it.

The house never got built and the foundation stood there for many years as a reminder of someone's fragmentary home.

Shortly after that, my parents separated and because of their devout Catholic upbringing, were able to secure an annulment. I always thought that made us three children out to be bastards.

Dad seemed nicer after that. He was limited to certain times and certain days and the sound of a car door at 4:30 PM meant Mom was coming home from her job. Her right hand was always reserved for embracing.

*Post Traumatic Stress Disorder

Chapter Two

New Life

Extreme Unction

I suppose it's understandable for a young girl to be confused about male authority when she's been beaten by her father, fondled by her uncle, and molested by her priest. What is even more understandable is to take all of this knowledge and store it away in the darkest closet of her mind and pretend it never happened. That's exactly what I did. Some things are just too awful to remember so I chose not to. But there were too many other body parts that *did* remember and it came out in behaviors that also are just too awful to remember. But unfortunately, I do.

As a result, I became an extremist; I formed a behavior and then overdid that behavior. I smoked too many cigarettes, drank too much beer, slept with too many men, and had a potty mouth. But I made the Dean's List. By the time I was twenty-six, I had quit going to college twice, immersed myself in the 60's hippie/peace community, traveled the country in search of myself and never found either myself or any of this peace we were all talking about.

My third time back in college was the charm. It was now the early seventies and I was about to graduate. I was easy to spot—I had grown out my naturally curly red hair and teased the life out of it into a huge afro. I always wore jeans on the bottom and whatever was conducive to the weather on the top. I moved into a house near the campus and watched a young man who lived in the downstairs apartment go through more stages of life than I had. When I met him, he was a nominal Catholic. Suddenly, halfway through his junior year, he had an epiphany that caused him to rearrange his bedroom to include a shrine. There he displayed an altar, incense, purple curtains, a kneeler, and a statue of Buddha. A few months into this, the term "Jesus Freak" started invading the house. The purple curtains came down and the Bible thumping came in.

"He's really done it this time," I thought. He wanted to tell me what happened and I didn't want to listen. I gave him "just this once" to talk to me. Sometimes once is all you need.

He was so new into the experience that the only road he knew how to travel was the Roman's Road. He shared it with me on a Saturday night that turned into a Sunday morning. Easter Sunday, to be exact. College students are wide awake at 2 am and it was somewhere around this time that I prayed a prayer with him and waited for the train whistles to blow and the clouds to part. That didn't happen.

What did happen was that my sincerity in praying planted a seed in my heart that began to blossom and bloom over the following week. I suppose the Spirit of the Lord had to come in gently and remove a lot of barriers located between my head and my heart. By the time Friday night came around, I had concluded that I must be a Christian. I'd spent the week repenting of my sins and stopping most of my bizarre behaviors. I began reading the Bible hungrily and crying at the drop of a hat. Mostly crying. It was the week before my college graduation and all my finals were that week. That I aced them all is comparable to the parting of the Red Sea. I graduated Magna Cum Laude with a BA that stood more for Born-Again.

I carried my extremist nature into the Kingdom with me. Just eight days later I was filled with the Holy Spirit with such force that a water balloon burst in my stomach and I fell to the ground. Okay, I was lying about the water balloon part but that's exactly the way it felt and I did fall to the ground. I had just read the Scripture the day before in John 7:38 that said "...out of his heart will flow rivers of living water," and I took it quite literally.

Without a doubt, I should have been one of those locked in that air-tight/no-light closet for a few months. Maybe not, though, because I led everything and everyone to the Lord, except maybe the family cat. Both my brothers and mother came to Christ within four months after I did. Looking back, it is obvious that I was both over-the-top and obnoxious about it, but the transformation process that took place was the greatest witness of all. Extreme was still working in my favor.

I lost nearly all my friends but I was okay with it. Many of us only shared camaraderie on a bar stool or sharing a joint. I was inhaling something new here—something so real it was worth the rejection and the change-in-life plans. In obedience to that new voice now coming from my heart, I told my university I would not be attending graduate school. I stayed where I was and waited for whatever was next. Within two years, "whatever" started happening and I found myself married to the pastor of my church.

Looking back, I see that most of what I learned after that took the form of on-the-job training.

Stars Struck

There's this desire in many of us that comes out of nowhere and it has to do with getting our fifteen minutes of fame. What it really comes from, more times than not, is a need to be accepted, acknowledged, and loved. We're human. It starts early in life. "Look what I just did!"

But sometimes that desire is so pressing we mistake it for our life quest and forget the reality that not everyone can make it to the top. Our twenty-first century world has distorted the perks of celebrity, whether we are actors or athletes, performers or politicians. We're fooled into believing success and recognition answer questions, provide solutions, promise popularity, promote peace, and always come with a big paycheck at the end of the week. We forget the short life-span that often comes attached to the climb. Worse, we carry our backpack on the hike and the weight of it, of yesterday's baggage, comes with us.

I was duped into believing my life could be better at the top of a self-constructed mountain and convinced myself that if I didn't make it on my own, I could grab hold of any shirttail I saw heading in that direction: up. In college, in my early twenties, I saw three such shirttails waving in the breeze and reached out to each of them to take me *there*—wherever *there* might be. Little did I know that my destiny was already shaped since the beginning of time and instead of believing I would arrive by climbing up, the Lord was more than pleased to step down and take me where I really needed to go.

Shirttail #1 — Climbing With Karen

My life-changing revelation of Jesus Christ came the week I was going to take a hit of speed with my friend, Karen. We wanted to see if we liked it. I think God knew I probably would like the drug, so He jumped right in there before that planned night and presented Himself to me in such a miraculous way that I suddenly had no desire for my old wild life. The change was that drastic, that quick, and that necessary. It was in 1973 and I became a true Jesus Freak—afro and all and, as mentioned, my die-hard Catholic mother was impressed enough to change her whole way of life. No one was able to scrape me off the ceiling for several months and by that time, I had led enough people to the Lord to really tick off the devil. Life, as I was now discovering, was good. I gave up graduate school and jumped heart-first into this new world.

Karen thought I was a whack job and tried the hit on her own.

She liked it.

She went on to become a well-known singer/dancer/entertainer. I don't know if she does drugs, though. I went to see her perform recently and she didn't remember who I was until I brought up the hit of speed we were supposed to share.

Shirttail #2 — Jacked Up

Jack was already a celebrity on local television and that was criteria enough for me to want a date with him. We only went out a couple of times when Jesus found my heart. The change

41

in me totally creeped him out and while our paths crossed a few times after that, he went on to host a nationally accredited television show, smoke entirely too much, and die of lung cancer at the age of 50. I saw him just six months before he died and wrote him a letter telling him about the Lord. I don't know if he read it or heeded it. I hope both.

Shirttail #3 — Talented Trevor

Trevor was one of my all-time favorite people. He was fun and kind and gifted as an actor. When I met him, he was doing local theatre, and I intentionally crashed the stage party so we could meet. He had the lead role, of course. After dating a few times, we settled on becoming good friends. I had no idea he was struggling with his own sexuality but I was happy enough just being his friend. He had great potential.

Two years into our friendship I became a Christian and portrayed all the obvious and obnoxious signs. I became louder and stranger and more overwhelming than the crazy red-headed college student he knew. Trevor was actually repelled by the change in me and said I reminded him of a possessed puppet on a string. Our relationship came to an abrupt end.

He went on to do bit parts in several well-known movies, made a guest appearance on the Oprah show, and succumbed to AIDS at the age of 41.

I think often about Karen and Jack and Trevor and my lust for celebrity.

I now realize being nameless and anonymous might just be a gift. Not all mountains are meant to be climbed.

Not at all odd, though, that I would marry my pastor.

Chapter Three
The Church

Starting From Scratch

Babes In Christ

The beginning of our church was earmarked by newly-saved and spirit-filled twenty-somethings hell-bent on a mission to save the rest of the world in the shortest amount of time possible. We embraced each other in such an intimate way that fellowship often got confused with dating. We were a band of extremists and fit right into the era of the Jesus Freaks and the liberated 70's. And being inordinately hungry, we devoured this new-found faith that allowed the Spirit-realm to open up and the love of God to come down.

And, yes, most of us should have been "closeted" for at least six months. But, personally, I think the Lord was pleased as all get-out with the whole lot of us. There was a sweet innocence about how we acted.

My own personal favorite part of the born-again experience was the miracle of becoming clean. What a privilege to obliterate the past and start life over with a clean slate. Born, absolutely, again.

Within the tiny timeframe of just two years, the younger generation among us began to meet in the living room of the youth pastor and eventually became a church unto themselves. My husband and I were asked to join the group and share in pastoral responsibilities. It grew so quickly that a third church was later formed from it. At this point, the majority of us who filled up that living room space were still babes in the Lord, though I'm sure many of us thought we'd gotten to the "young man" stage. We were all pretty much in need of some guidance and my husband began to do just that—to guide us.

It was a good start on a good road with good intentions.

Legs To Stand On

For several years, the church grew rapidly from "within" as God said, "Be fruitful and multiply," and everyone replied, "Amen, Lord," and all the babies started coming. However, because we lived in a college town, we grew just as rapidly from "without." Newly converted college students began attending the church, and we babes in Christ were now becoming first-time parents, both in the natural and in the spirit. Our spiritual adolescence never stopped us from growing and maturing, and our continued appetites allowed us to gulp down all the right spiritual nourishment to keep ourselves and our souls replenished and healthy.

We were a hearty bunch. Lives were being changed, hearts were softening to the Gospel and we were attracting attention—the right kind—in the community. Until—

Until we got off just a fraction of an inch, and a fraction of an inch is a fraction of an inch too far. Miles down the road, the gap widens, and the view back from that distance becomes blurred and, eventually, unrecognizable. By that time, where you came from is out of sight and forgotten. And I think that's what happened to us. I think we got ourselves a bad case of spiritual amnesia.

Many lost were still getting saved and experiencing profound transformation, prayer meetings and sermons were still vibrant, the anointing during worship and on visiting prophets was still palpable, but it was what we did in our personal relating and council and admonition—how we helped people grow spiritually—that veered in the wrong direction.

We got sin-conscious. We got image-conscious. We got self-conscious.

We were balancing on a tripod of consciousness that couldn't support the church structure without, at some point, collapsing in on itself.

Joint Replacment

I recently went to a foot doctor with a complaint that the big toe on my right foot was traveling north and making holes in my socks. The fact that I could only wear sandals was a problem. It was winter. X-rays showed that the two-sectioned artificial joint put in there over 25 years ago (by a now-retired doctor) had separated and the top joint would need to be replaced.

I had the surgery done and within a period of just a few months, watched my big toe fall down on itself, becoming increasingly shorter, distressingly wider and finally resembling a tiny Buddha with a nail for a head. The doctor told me that was normal. I didn't like her definition of normal and went for a second opinion. New x-rays showed that the top joint had indeed been removed but was never replaced with a healthy substitute. The toe didn't have a "leg" to stand on and could only do what gravity allowed it to do—collapse onto itself.

The affects of collapsing are much more far-reaching and devastating for a church than for a toe.

Sin-Cerely

Sin conscious. I'm still not sure why sin became such a fixation for us, but the obsession we developed with it initiated that fraction of an inch departure from wholeness. Perhaps because so many of us came into the Kingdom heavy laden in the sin department, we saw sin as something that needed to be first discerned and then dealt with right away.

And by saying that, I'm not denying sin's existence or its repulsion or its devastating potential. There are definitely times when it needs to be confronted. Seeing sin in others is easy; whether or not to address their sin takes discernment; how to address the sin takes wisdom. More often than not, it is just a signal for us to take what we've been shown and bring it to our knees in prayer.

At some point, we confused this focus with the simplicity of merely having a relationship with another brother or sister in Christ.

At some point, we crossed over from spiritualizing to scrutinizing, to setting up our antennae, pointing our divining rods, holding out our Geiger Counters.

At some point, we lost the point. We searched out sin and confronted it head-on. We failed to realize it had already been confronted head-on about two thousand years ago. Or else we just forgot.

It was a diversion, a gradual one, and we never really understood just how dangerous this practice was. It was a distraction from the enemy, hidden under the guise of "rescuing" our brothers and sisters in Christ, helping them grow, pointing out what we saw that they didn't see that needed "fixing."

In actuality, it was our beam and their sliver.

Beaming In

We're an imperfect people learning to welcome a perfect Godhead into the affairs of an imperfect world. You only have to read about the Israelites and their capacity to go to and fro in their devotion to God to see how easily we can walk away from Him, but also how desperately we need Him.

By sending us Jesus, sin was already dealt with at the time of our spiritual rebirth. The work was already accomplished—we just had to come into agreement with it. The atonement was done, complete, finished. Our only real "job," after discovering the joy of knowing this, was to encourage one another in that truth. And to learn so much more about who this Jesus really is and what this Jesus really did and what He is still trying to do.

I have since come to a place where I firmly believe that our obsession with sin issues was actually a manifestation of something far worse and more deep-seated than anything we labeled as sin. It was actually within the leadership that this sin issue got so completely out of hand. It crippled us, making us unable to know and walk in our true identity in Christ.

49

Understanding the breadth, width, and depth of His Love and Truth will take up the entire rest of my lifetime. It should take up everyone else's time, as well.

Adolescent Elders

The newly formed eldership consisted of young men in their early- to mid-twenties who were, in a real sense, still babes in Christ themselves. This was a pretty common practice among many of the new works that were springing up around America at that time. The Jesus movement poured forth a slew of us who never lacked the necessary energy but somewhat lacked the necessary maturity. Some of those positions were filled, it seemed, by the more "popular" men. And, yes, they were all filled by men.

It reminded me of high school and how we went about choosing who would be the senior class president or the student council representative. Too many of us turned them into popularity contests and at our church we may have been duped by that same concept. Once elected, and here's where it gets scary, position and title somehow became the mandate for ruling the roost. I would know: I was viewing it, or so I surmised, from the top. I was three years into walking with the Lord and I was the pastor's wife. While I was never allowed a ministry outside of heading the women's ministry within the church, I was as confident in my ruling powers as any of the men.

We sincerely believed we were hand-picked by the Lord Himself to possess the necessary wisdom and insight for the rest of the people. Most especially, it was the senior pastor who had the vision, the heart, and the power.

I have no problem with pastors having vision and heart. I have a problem with what they do with the power part. I have a problem with the abuse of said power. It marked the beginning of the second leg on the tripod stool—we became image-conscious.

Image-In That

Having a hierarchy within the church seemed to be one of those unwritten rules and those unwritten rules were multiplying themselves on a regular basis. For every failure or weakness or misunderstanding, we set up a rule. We used the Word to back up every law we made. That's an easy thing to do—the enemy loves to help us twist the Word by whatever angle we come from and whatever belief we support. We need His Spirit with us when we study the Word—we're far too flawed, far too prejudiced, far too deceived to interpret it on our own.

Coming from such sin-filled backgrounds, one would think it would have created within us more of an empathy for those with flaws, but it seemed to create more of a comparison. It seemed to provide us with a dividing line between ruler and ruled. I know, on a personal basis, it made me feel better about my own weaknesses, which I had now been admonished were not to be demonstrated before others. It was important that we look good if this is going to be the position we held. Above.

As leaders, we were not immune from sin, but our sin issues needed to be kept under wraps. We entered, it seemed, our own witness protection program. It's important that you look good. That's what the Christian witness is all about, isn't it? Looking good to the outside world. Jesus must be glorified, right? We had to do that for Him, right? Besides, the pastor has been working overtime to help out the flock and it really does reflect back on him just how effective his work has been. So looking good is important.

Picture the idyllic family as they pose for that glossy photograph that will don the front of this year's Christmas card. They're dressed in their finest outfits, usually bearing the standard shades of red and green, their hair is perfectly coifed and everyone is smiling. One-after-another, the pictures are taken until everyone looks their best, all in that one split second of time, and that becomes the picture that adorns the card. No one but the family knows about the fight they had on the way to the studio, the porn the kids were watching on-line the night before, or the impending divorce the parents are planning to announce after the holidays are over.

That's a little bit like what was going on at church. What made us act like everything was just fine when it wasn't? What kept us from being real? At what point did we start to get so religious that we thought we all needed to look good?

When does a Pharisee become a Pharisee—when we don a white robe or when we harden our heart? Or do these things happen at the same time? Does the robe come on in direct proportion to the heart hardening? I use the collective word "we" here because I am guilty; I am a Pharisee in rehab.

It became important that we looked good from the outside, too—the side the unsaved are watching. Heaven forbid the church be filled with the dregs of sin. Heaven forbid it be known that the people of God struggle with their own infirmities or addictions or wrongdoings, or any of us evidence an obvious flaw that might make Jesus look bad.

But by this time we had forgotten that very simple fact: heaven *doesn't* forbid it. Heaven *embraces* it.

As long as we kept looking good from the outside, all went well. We were the front of the Christmas card. But the front of a Christmas card is not real—it is a mere image; it is two dimensional. We were losing who we really were by masking our weaknesses and showing a false self to our church family. The church is not a triangle with kings and queens at the top. It is a circle without a circumference. It is the Body of Christ with only one Head. All the parts had a need for each other but we were afraid to allow ourselves to be ourselves, and we couldn't see what we truly were—to ourselves or to each other.

Within my own home, the rules mounted as I became increasingly and outwardly flawed. I shopped too often, talked too much, and had an interesting variety of unhealthy fears balanced with a few silly obsessions. So more Carol-specific rules were added, in addition to all the other rules, and soon I was trapped in a small circle with big rules. Religion had taken its toll. Religion is tiny and binding; it keeps real healing—at-the-root healing—at bay. Within my heart, within my home, and within the church, I stopped growing.

Over the years, by the grace of God, our church continued to grow. We were strengthened by outside ministries that would

come in and bring the Word of God in power. We allowed the prophetic word to encourage us in Presbytery meetings. Fellowship blossomed and new relationships grew. In other words, we evidenced outward signs of a healthy church.

Inwardly, though, we continued to discern the sin in others and polish up the outside of the vessel.

Our third leg was the most wobbly of all, and the scariest.

Ex-Aulted

We actually believed we exemplified 21st century Christianity before that new century arrived. We were God's example of what the church should look like. We saw ourselves as a church demonstrating to the outside world the *cutting edge* of the move of God. All we were waiting for was some kind of national recognition.

Of course, we didn't say this from the pulpit, nor was it written down in our confession of faith. But we spoke of it amongst ourselves and looked forward to the day others would see what we saw.

Only we saw amiss. We were deceived.

In a way, I see the irony to this tripod of flimsy fabric—our best and firmest tripod would and should have been the Trinity, but even the belief in the Trinity had been squashed by the leadership as being heresy.

Years later, I told the Lord how sorry I was we broke Him up that way. He said He could handle it. He'd already been crucified.

Sacred Scars

I don't believe stories like mine of my church experiences are limited to just my own church body. I have seen the same things happen all around me in multitudes of churches. They most certainly start off on that same good road with those same good intentions.

*"The road to hell is paved with good intentions,"** is often used by people who have withdrawn themselves from the rules and regulations of their religious upbringing. And I suppose I could be presumptuous and say that all of us came out from under this legalism bearing scars. We need to be real, we need to tell our stories, and we need to heal.

The scars Jesus bears are intentional scars. He displayed them and He wore them on purpose. Our scars were inflicted on us by church people we have loved. They can best be described as being the result of friendly fire. No one meant to kill or maim on purpose, but we did shoot arrows of accusation at each other and God's people got hurt and some of them even died.

"Father forgive us for we knew not what we were doing."

We would succumb to our injuries were it not for divine intervention that brought about divine healing. Those of us who bear scars and have been resurrected from what should have killed us, should display these scars by stretching out our hands to all the Thomas's who want to touch them.

Scars should show others where we came from, but should not be the basis for where we are going.

* No one knows for sure who the author is of this well-known proverb.

More Unwritten Rules

I gave up Christmas trees for ten years because they were false gods.

The Easter Bunny laid its last egg in my house.

The Cabbage Patch doll my daughter got from her aunt became one with the garbage can to keep her 11-month-old mind from exhibiting a spirit of pride.

I gave away all my beautiful earrings because each one of those holes in my lobes was a disgrace.

We worked through all these rules, broke through them, and eventually broke out of them. But new ones surfaced.

The local bookstore sold all kinds of books, including the Bible we attributed to God as well as the one that satan wrote. We took our book needs elsewhere.

The local coffee shop was owned by a hippie and drew a like crowd. We met anywhere else for coffee.

After the bus crash,* the main places I frequented were the local bookstore and the coffee shop owned by the hippie. I never ran into church people there so they became safe havens for me. They were also great places to express the love of the Lord, which I did, and frequently, over the last few years.

Father, forgive us for not knowing what to do but doing the wrong thing, anyway.

* Described in the introduction.

On The Line

Hot Line

We had a 24-hour Hot Line that people who wanted prayer could call. I signed up for a midnight detail. Nobody wanted the 10 PM to 6 AM shift but I liked the idea of spending the night on the bed they put in the room and not having to take a lot of calls. So that became my once-a-week shift and I slept pretty well. The fact that I was only months old in the Lord didn't seem to bother anybody.

I think they mistook passion for spiritual maturity.

Anyway, I remember one unusual evening getting one phone call after another from a woman who was saying something that even I won't dare repeat on paper; it was THAT blasphemous. The man who would soon be my husband walked into the room as I was dealing with call number three and began to pray for me. When she called a fourth time, he took the call, rebuked the hell out of her and hung up. The phone was silent the rest of the night and I began to consider the man a spiritual giant.

I think I mistook passion for spiritual maturity.

Date Line

A year later we were married. I knew while we were dating he was absolutely the right man for me. I could be myself and not try to impress him. (That would be short-lived). The hardest thing for me to work through was the fact that he had been married before and had a daughter, but since his divorce was for the "right Scriptural reason," I believed I was doing the right thing.

He had married at 19, she was 17 and they had a little girl four years later. She would be their only child. At the age of 25, he came to know the Lord and immediately started attending Bible College while working full-time at night to support his family. His wife wanted nothing to do with either his new-found faith or his new lifestyle and by the time he graduated, they were divorced and she had new boyfriends.

No one comes into the Kingdom without carrying at least an overnight bag. Some of us, though, have luggage.

I believed our marriage would work. I believed I would love him to my dying day. Yet, even when our own divorce happened, some thirty years later, I still believed marrying him was the will of God for me. God's will is only broken by our own will. His second divorce was not, shall we say, for the "right Scriptural reason" nor was it my desire. I was foolish enough to think we might be able to work it out. I see now—ah, hindsight—it was more of a rescue plan for me.

Blood Line

The early years were good ones. We worked well as a team and enjoyed having a wonderful group of church people as our friends. I did all the wifely things and submitted to my role as Pastor's wife. I also submitted to his definition of submission and never thought much about it. There was an order to keep and I kept it, though occasionally straying when I knew I was right and he didn't. Ok, so maybe occasionally is not the right word. But I know and remember we were happy and recall there were only two real concerns in our lives. One we shared within the intimacy of our home and marriage; the other I dared not share with him at all. But both, regrettably, I internalized to a fault. Internalizing was all I could do. Many Pastor's wives, this one included, have no one to go to and no one to share with; at least, no one with skin on who wasn't already part of the local church community.

The first concern was my inability to get pregnant. Over the years, it shifted from a monthly concern to a daily concern and got to be an unhealthy obsession for me. I called my periods "red tears" and struggled to watch the flock expand as all my friends conceived and birthed child after child. My vision of a loving Father began to diminish. I knew the source of life and He wasn't putting any in me, and I questioned His love when He knew darn well how much I wanted to have babies of my own. We struggled with this for nearly nine years and while adoption put an end to much of the outward pain, the internal damage was never really addressed until decades later. By then it had time to settle in my soul. Internal deposits never really go away. They stay. They fester.

Head Line

My other concern related to my husband's ministry, especially as he rose in stature to the position of senior pastor and believed he was on the way to becoming an apostle. At first, I attributed his not having close male friends as just part of the job. He was so busy running a church and being a husband and a father. But quietly in my heart, I wanted to believe such a man existed who could truly be his friend, who might be able to speak things into his life. You don't have to be married long to realize your spouse isn't fond of correction, especially if he's in a "power" position. I became increasingly frustrated to discover no real "male bonding" taking place within the church eldership, which became my last, best hope. What I did see only mimicked intimacy; the common denominator was that all the men who gathered around him agreed with him. Even when he introduced mandatory head-coverings be worn by all the women in the church or the concept that the Trinity did not, in fact, ever even exist, except in the imagination of men, the men would all nod in agreement. My husband rarely listened to anything I brought up that were house/marriage/family issues; I didn't dare consider introducing church issues into the mix. I was, after all, female.

Any man, in or out of ministry, who crossed the line and attempted to oppose, suggest, or confront him on any of his decision-making was met with a firm rebuke.

He had heard from God.

How dare you?

It was perhaps a dozen years later before I discovered others *had* tried to talk to him. All this time, I had thought I was the only one to recognize the need. It was a hard load to carry, but I was told I had to; it was part of the definition of the Christian "S" word - submission.

Flat Line

I hate to tell this story. It's embarrassing.

It was 1999 and unless you hid yourself away in a fallout shelter, you knew something terrible might happen when all those computers turned that four-digit year into 2000 at the stroke of midnight, December 31st. My husband was one of the doomsday gang and had me storing canned goods and barrels of drinking water in the basement for most of the year. He warned us all from the pulpit. He stood firm in his conviction, as he had with all his convictions.

January 1st came and went. Without incident, as we all know.

I guess I thought maybe he would say he made a mistake or he was sorry or he got fooled, but it was like nothing happened. He never talked about it, either at home or from the pulpit, and my heart began to ache as I saw a man, my man, unable to even admit he had made a mistake.

This is something I have come to know that is so terribly mandatory in the Kingdom—you make a mistake and now you're sorry. The confession we make, facing truth because we really do screw up pretty regularly, has to be one of the most humbling

of acts we humans are instructed to do. But it is also a privilege, actually, because the reward is so liberating. We are forgiven each and every time. And we become a better person for it.

As this state of mind continued in him, I saw something sinister happening. I call it *arrogance* now, but at the time, I only called it *stubbornness*. Being stubborn can, later on, produce arrogance.

There was a time when I became so frustrated I blurted out: *"How did you make it past the repentant part when you got saved?"*

He walked out of the room. Of course.

Underline

Why should that story embarrass me? This is the one that should.

"The law kills, but the Spirit gives life." Apparently I had misunderstood this word. Law after law was placed upon me as a way of changing me to be whatever it was I wasn't. For each one of my flaws, a new law was applied for me to follow. When that law didn't change me, the only conclusion reached was that I did not love God, or I was a Jezebel or demon-possessed or, my personal favorite, I was just not saved to begin with.

At this point in my marriage, I was told who could and could not be my friends and what I could and could not buy at the store. As each new restraint was applied, I felt myself becoming increasingly paralyzed in that part of me that was, well, me.

Living under the law for so long was also affecting my speech. Whenever I thought it necessary to say something to my husband, even something irrelevant, I discovered my throat would close up and I wouldn't be able to get the words out. It was as if there were something around my neck, like a noose or maybe even a snake of sorts, and it kept me from being able to speak.

I had an undergraduate degree in communication and now a graduate degree in writing—I know how to get something across. But not to him. Not to the one I was supposed to be One with.

And maybe that was the problem.

Father, forgive him, he knew not what he was doing. And neither did I.

Deadline

My freezer stopped freezing, which wasn't that much of a big deal since we lived in a duplex and our neighbor was the landlord. He came by and transferred our food into his own freezer. Within a day or two, he fixed the problem and loaded our freezer back up with more than we had taken out. His marijuana brownies found their way into my freezer, unnoticed and unlabeled. I served them to company the next night.

I love brownies. I have always loved brownies the best and probably more than cookies. My mother had a recipe that she called Fudge Bars and they were still a brownie but had the consistency of fudge. The batter was better than the brownie itself and there were times when my best friend in high school and I would make up the brownie batter and split it evenly, eating the uncooked batter with a spatula while we listened to a Johnny Mathis album and day-dreamed of getting married, having children and serving the cooked renditions to company. We didn't know about salmonellae then and if we did, we wouldn't have cared in the same way my friend's teenage daughter doesn't care to stop texting while she drives on the highway.

My company included a chocoholic who ate four brownies and the rest of us used diplomacy and limited ourselves to one. Two of us were unaffected. My friend and I, however, took off; he traveled a lot farther and a lot faster and a lot longer. I, on the other hand, went just far enough to go out of my mind for several unnerving hours.

Pastor's wives, for the most part, do not take illegal drugs.

Four gallons of water and twelve hours later, my friend and I were back to normal. It would be another month before we learned about the landlord's error in shipping and by then I had already miscarried. It was my only pregnancy.

Section Two

Break Out

"...I will break his yoke from your neck and will burst your bonds..."

Jeremiah 30:8b

Chapter Four

Insights
Coming In

I've Got You Covered

The new head-covering revelation I was about to receive began to painstakingly unfold as I sat in the front row of the conference room, listening to the woman speaker discuss the eleventh chapter of 1st Corinthians. All the women around me, myself included, were wearing doilies or small veils on the backs of our heads. We were told this was an outward sign that we were in submission to our husbands. If we were single, it signified we were under the authority of a male figure-head within the church body. I am not sure why the women felt they needed to do this, but I knew I had to. I was married to the senior pastor, the one with the original revelation we women were all adhering to. I had been waiting a long time for my own revelation of truth to happen regarding this matter and it never did, but I submissively obeyed anyway. Until now. Because now I was listening to a woman tell me the very opposite of what it was I was forced into believing and doing and I liked what I was hearing.

A lot.

"Dear God, I must be rebellious," was my first thought.

"Dear God, this is wonderful, liberating news," was my second thought.

I hung on to both thoughts for a long time, regarding this and a lot of other matters that would come up again in the future.

The conference room was too large for the number of women it held, so the chairs were set up within a smaller space in the middle of the room, leaving wide aisles around and in back of the chairs. The speaker was overly animated (I liked this, as well)

69

and she began to encircle the chairs in a dramatic fashion as she shared with us that a head covering was not physical but spiritual in meaning. I can only imagine what was going on in her mind as she sashayed around to the back of the conference room and got a new perspective of her audience.

From her new vantage point, she could easily see that all our heads were dotted in white lace doilies.

Removing The Veil

I came home later in the day than the other women because the pastor's wife has to settle the bill and make sure the ladies left with everything they brought. "Retreats" came to be known as "Advances," since none of us wanted to believe we were going backwards. I was excited to share the liberating, "forwarding" news with my husband. It was also our wedding anniversary and we had made plans to go out to dinner that night.

The news didn't take long to reach his ears. Many of the other women had shared the head-covering teaching with their own husbands and the speaker's sacrilegious sermon was immediately reported to mine.

It was the last time she was ever allowed to come to our church.

I was barely into the first sentence of sharing my revelation when he threw my present at me, mumbled "Happy Anniversary," and walked out of the room.

I thanked the Lord it was a blouse and not a crock-pot.

All I remember eating for dinner that night was crow.

But I also remember feeling entirely right about something. It was a new feeling.

I liked it.

A lot.

Foundations

"Hate to bother you guys, but would you take down a sheet or two of the paneling in your basement? I need to see what's going on with your foundation."

We had hired this man to put in a couple of French drains around the house because water from storms and melting snow would gather in puddles around the house and we wanted it as far removed from the foundation as possible. So when he came to the door to ask us this question, we knew something must be terribly wrong. The man was an engineer by profession; putting in French drains was a hobby. His engineer eye saw something bigger than a slanted landscape; he saw a slanted foundation.

What we had was a 1700 square-foot ranch with a basement ready to cave in because it had been built with shoddy materials, no reinforcement rods and smack-dab in the middle of a wet zone. The cost to fix the problem—rebuild the basement and redo the landscaping—began a journey that would end in a divorce, a church split, a divided family, and multitudes of broken relationships within the house of the Lord.

71

Other than that, once the broken bricks and junk were taken out, a new foundation was laid, and all our savings were depleted because the statute of limitation was up and we couldn't sue the prior owners, our old house was like new.

The house of the Lord, on the other hand, takes a tad longer to repair. Living stones have a tendency to crawl away from unstable foundations. I would know that for a fact because I was about to crawl out myself.

Crumbling Cornerstone

Once the paneling came down and the truth was exposed, we surveyed the basement and gasped. There were large, gaping holes in the foundation where stone or brick should have been. Pieces of wood, aluminum foil or globs of wood putty had been wedged between the openings by the previous, and only, owners of the house. The paneled basement concealed the horror but never, of course, solved the problem. We had discovered a number of other hidden items that needed fixing since moving into that house, but never to the extent that this one presented. It was possible that it could have caused severe damage or worse, a sudden death.

Instead, it brought on a long, slow, drawn-out one.

The local building inspector cancelled earlier plans to do other jobs in the neighborhood using large machinery; the vibrations from them, he feared, would have caused the whole structure to collapse. The cornerstone of the house suffered the most damage, evidenced by the broken and crumbling pieces of brick that lay where the strength of the whole house should have been.

The cornerstone was just beneath the master bedroom, where we had slept night after night. We lay unaware that just beneath us, what should have been supporting us was, in reality, for the most part, non-existent.

Shortly after this discovery, a young man approached my husband with the usual fear most church members experienced when they wanted to say something to him.

"Do you think maybe the Lord was trying to tell you something and is using what happened to your foundation to say it?"

My husband quickly snapped back, "*Of course not!*"

The 'V' Word

"I FEEL SO VIOLATED!"

That was all I could say, over and over, as the situation unfolded, as the basement and landscaping were removed and the monies flew out the window.

Violated.

It was a new word for me and it seemed more important than any word I spoke. It kept entering into conversation. It was the only word that described how I was feeling.

Somehow, I had been violated before and it was this event and this word that opened up a part of a past of which I had no previous memory.

73

I began to realize it wasn't the first time I had been violated and a certain uncle's face soon invaded my mind. I called his only living sibling and asked, with layers of apology preceding the question: "Do you happen to know if your brother ever molested anybody?"

To which she replied: "Oh, no, honey, YOU TOO?"

The head covering revelation occurred at the exact same time as the basement instability was discovered. These two occurrences marked the exact point at which I can say my life and our marriage began a downward tumble.

Stain Remover

I sat straight up in bed, eyes wide open, heart pounding. I went into the kitchen and wrote out as many details as I could recall about the dream I'd just had. It was nearly 4 AM and the energy surging through me would keep me up the rest of the day. I knew the Lord was trying to tell me something because of the way it was weighing on me. Heavily. The events in the dream seemed almost dull, so it should have come and gone as most dreams do. But it was in 3-D Technicolor, High Definition with surround sound.

It was a simple enough request. Would my husband please clean that large stain in the middle of the living room carpet while I was out doing chores? It was a huge black stain and must have measured at least three or four feet in diameter. It was round and dark against the light blue carpeting and it was unsightly. It needed to be removed immediately, before it set in, before the flooring might have to be replaced, before it would prove costly.

When I arrived home, I asked my husband if he cleaned the stain and did it come out and he assured me yes he had and yes it did. I went into the living room and realized he had not removed the stain at all. He'd merely rearranged the living room furniture so that the stain was no longer visible. The new furniture arrangement, I couldn't help but notice, was no longer conducive to conversation.

It wasn't removed – it was camouflaged.

I have never had a dream that pierced my heart so deeply.

A few nights later, I awoke with another ever-so-vivid, shocking dream to work through. It was about the men in our church eldership. I didn't know it at the time, but it was a dire warning from God of what was to come.

Old men dream dreams. Old women do, too, I suppose. Mine were put down in my journal, in detail, and then placed in His hands for many years. I wasn't going to try and figure them out.

Time and circumstance and the discovery of hidden sin did that for me.

Revelation unveils itself over time, as you will see.

Discerning Of Spirits

Two men of God were flown to our church from two different states and were paid to counsel and pray over the Eldership and their wives. My husband had conveniently scheduled himself to be out of the country at that time and let me know he was just fine without their prayers but it would be good for me to get some. I was in desperate need of a touch from the Lord and sought Him diligently before meeting with them.

My search led me, strangely enough, to do a detailed study of the word *occult*. It's definition, relating to and involving witchcraft, along with something that was *hidden* or *kept secret*, brought me to my knees and I sought the Lord further, asking Him to please show me what more evil was lurking in my heart and please please please rip it out by the roots so I could be a better wife.

I poured out my heart and my sins and my past and my newly discovered convictions and lay them on the table before these men. I confessed I was probably hanging on to something evil from the past that would not let go of me, something that was keeping me from being the kind of wife my husband was expecting me to be. I didn't know what that something was but surely it was lying there, infecting me. I had spent years and years repenting of multiple sins multiple times before. Perhaps I had missed something in my sin search and it just needed to be identified and dealt with.

They listened intently and allowed me to go beyond the scheduled time frame with my blabbering.

I was, after all, the *Senior* Pastor's wife.

Their method of counsel included sending me back to the waiting room, while the two of them discussed both me and my situation. Then they would bring me back in for sound advice, a spirit-led resolution, and the concluding prayer.

They called me back within ten minutes. The two men looked at me and then at each other. The louder of the two men of God leaned over the table and put his ruddy face into mine, well past that place and space where you know the comfort level has been crossed. He looked me straight in the eye as he firmly but kindly spoke these words,

"I think your husband is weird."

The rest of that meeting was a blur as they went on to expose what was really being hidden from me, that they were not my sins or offenses at all and that it was not my burden to carry them or blame myself for what was going on. They were the sins of another. What *was* my burden was to take this knowledge of the truth and carry it in silence. I was never to tell a soul what they had just told me, which I found to be a greater burden than the imagined sin itself.

I tried carrying it around for a couple of years, but the weight of it began to break me from within. I made a poor silent martyr and it was many years later before I realized the burden was not mine to bear but to share.

While this might have been the greatest discerning of a situation, it was the lousiest piece of wisdom I'd ever been given. And yes, I know, I just now broke a promise and it thrills my soul to do it. Makes me want to put a smiley face at the end of this story. ☺

Tattle Tails

This is not the first time I've let secrets go. In the past, I talked entirely too much. What I should not have been talking about were the things I was told to keep in my "Ponder Pocket." That's the place Mary stored everything she saw and heard. It's best to put them away and bring them out for the right occasion.

But I had a hard time finding that delicate balance. I struggled so much to be *me* and to be approved by God.

Talking too much (and too loud) was one of the "sins" I was so often accused of, but it wasn't just my mouth that got me into trouble.

We ladies were having a grand old time at the Women's Advance, paying no attention to the rustic surroundings and the bunk beds we were forced to climb into at night. What mattered was that we were together, away from the ordinary, and enjoying each other's fellowship.

The first morning at breakfast, sitting around one of many large circular tables in the dining area, one of the ladies asked me for a roll. I threw myself on the floor and rolled over, something I probably would not be able to do today without help.

The ladies roared.

Earlier that year, I was walking in a mall with my daughter, who was just three years old. A crowd of shoppers had gathered around a large fuzzy rabbit, and I suddenly remembered it was Easter week. I had forgotten about the dreaded bunny rabbit. My daughter was desperate to see what was going on and I gave in to her. We waited in line for the lap-sitting. I rarely frequented this mall and I was sure I was safe, until I saw the sister of a church member get in the line right behind me. We chatted briefly, my daughter told the rabbit Jesus loved him (or her) and we went home.

I got called into the church office for both these incidents, the rabbit and the rolling, and was thoroughly chastised for my rebelliousness. What especially concerned the leadership was the poor example I was setting as the wife of a pastor, for the church, as well as the unsaved.

I believed their accusation that I was rebellious, and I dutifully repented. Now I know I was just being human.

Just recently, a lovely man of God told me, "I always thought you were a size 8 foot jammed into a size 4 shoe."

Mind Alteration

I wasn't changing the way he wanted me to change, *he* being my husband.

The acting and the imitating weren't cutting it. The change wasn't happening. Whatever the standard was, I apparently wasn't meeting it.

I laughed too loud and lacked tact in some situations. I interrupted people who were talking because I suddenly had something to say and didn't give them a chance to finish what they were saying. I looked for ways to find compliments from people so I would feel better about myself. I was prideful on so many levels and just as insecure at the same time. Worse yet, I was more than aware of all these faults and frailties of mine.

I tried so hard to change, knowing none of them looked good, not good at all, and reflected poorly on my husband and the church. The church, after all, was supposed to look good; that was the determining factor of its success, a reflection of the good work the pastor had done. I was screwing up royally.

Hindsight is wonderful. I have it now, and I see and understand the transformation process, but I didn't have hindsight then and I only knew how to act or imitate.

My husband told me to see my doctor and get on medication and maybe it would help make me become what it was he was looking for. Perfection, perhaps?

Stepford wife came to mind. I'd seen both versions of the movie, *The Stepford Wives.* An idyllic Connecticut neighborhood was the setting for a grand scheme take-over of all the wives who lived there. Their frightening submission to their husbands turned them into robotic creatures, unable to think for themselves. They did everything their husbands demanded and never spoke back. The husbands were knit together in the scheme and one-by-one, the women succumbed to the take-over.

That most certainly was not MY idea of perfection. I didn't think it was what the Lord had in mind, either.

But I wanted so much to be better and to be a good wife. I had no idea that my own past abuses were compounded by living under another kind of abuse. I would think it was an oxymoron to pin "spiritual" and "abuse" side-by-side in the same sentence.

I went to see my doctor and was given Prozac and a follow-up appointment six weeks later. After eight days, I sensed the inside of my head hazing out and taking me to a place I wasn't willing to visit. The tug to get me someplace else was so strong, I was afraid I might not be able to resist it very long. It reminded me of a drowning person losing that sense of sheer panic and surrendering, finally, to the death process. I called the doctor and asked if I could take myself off the Prozac without having withdrawal. He gave the okay and soon I found my head again. It was a far more comfortable place than where I appeared to be heading.

Apparently, my husband did not like my head and commented, "I liked you better on Prozac."

Good. Then take some yourself and maybe you might like me just as I am.

Drug Test

Yes, I know it works for some people. Yes, I know some of you take some yourself and praise Him for it every day. Yes, I know it might be the will of God but no, it doesn't work for me.

Besides, how would I know when I'm better? Because better is what I wanted to be.

Boxed Up

There they sit—three sturdy brown boxes that once housed a shipment of Kodak film and now encase all the details and dialogues of a woman and her God. These are my journals and my stories as I see them.

Go ahead, open one at random and read it aloud to anyone. I won't be embarrassed: my journals are my journey; a painful journey at times, but like a good who-done-it, it's filled with twists and turns, break-ups and break-downs, and—more importantly—break-throughs.

For my own use, they certainly detail a lot of BEFORE AND AFTER pictures. Sure, I cringe a lot at the way I perceived something and expressed it on paper. Down the road, a few years and a whole lotta lessons later, I see things differently because I have changed. In essence, my mind has been renewed. It's all very Scriptural and nothing to apologize for.

It took me a while to see all that, to not carry around blame and shame when it wasn't warranted.

People can be really paranoid about journals. They're not ashamed to say they keep one, but they don't want anyone reading them. They say journals are private matters of the heart. They argue that they ought to stay right where they are—hidden— never to be shared with anyone.

So let me ask: who is it you're writing to, anyway? If you just want to write for the sake of writing, you have only yourself to construct this correspondence with, a "Dear Diary" kind of thing. But if you're a Christian, the journals can reflect a written intimacy with the Lord.

I thoroughly believe I am writing to the Lord. I like the idea that He can speak back to me and put my heart and His word back together again. For so long, my heart was so wide open with need that I didn't bother wearing it on my sleeve—I hung it on my face so it was the first thing you saw. That wasn't necessarily a good thing, but before that, in the early stages of the journey, my journal entries were sincere. My face, on the other hand, was another read entirely.

One entry reads:

"I am beginning to see who I really am and I am uglier and far less a woman than I ever imagined...I am weak and insecure and arrogant, unable to cope ... There is no place of prominence in my life. I won't be on any cereal box cover and I won't have a chance to speak to 2,000 people at a clip and I won't write anything anyone would pay money for."

I was trying to be the cooperating wife; okay, the submissive wife. I was trying to keep it together, to keep my marriage together, to remember Who it was I really belonged to, that my worth was found in Christ and not in a man. But I was feeling like, what did they call them? Oh, yes, a Stepford wife. Taken over and made into perfection. Robotic.

I related this Stepford revelation to a pastor friend I loved as deeply as a brother.

I was thoroughly rebuked and told to never say that again.

But I just did, didn't I?

I told you because I now know it was healthy to confront it and name it and see it for what it was: *un*healthy. And certainly not God.

I was being programmed into some kind of mechanical helpmate. I was also instructed about who I was to be friends with and learned, years after the divorce, that my husband had approached some of my friends and told them not to be friends with me anymore. To top it off, I was told to stay silent about my feelings and, as it seemed was now happening, I had no other choice but to allow the process to overtake me.

Sounds exactly like a Stepford wife, doesn't it?

Introduction To Misogamy

I will never forget about the pastor's wife with the carrot-red hair. Actually, it was more like highly-greased hair closer in color to copper. She strutted down the church aisle and made her way to the piano of the church we were visiting. There was something about her, more than just the hair, that made everyone take notice. You wouldn't have recognized anything unusual about her if you just listened to her play. She played well. Very well.

But she was off somehow. Not normal. It took one dinner out with the pastor and his wife to know something was terribly wrong with her. Her husband had to cut her meat for her and spoke with her as if he were conversing with a child. It was a little awkward and, worse for us, happened without explanation. We were left to speculate.

We were never in touch with this couple again, but looking back, I suspect the poor woman had either a brain tumor or a case of dementia.

But that was not what my husband saw and pointed it out to me very plainly on the way home.

"That's exactly what happens to a pastor's wife when she stops having a relationship with the Lord and depends on her husband's ministry to carry her through."

It was followed by a mini-sermon on submission.

Two Crazies

I was chatting with a woman whose husband used to be an elder at my old church. She told me there was a meeting of the elders and their wives immediately following the "bus crash." The associate pastor announced to the group that I was crazy. That was his exact word. Crazy.

My first response was that it bothered the hell out of me. Hell, out of me, is a good thing. Attitude is quite another.

My other, kinder and grace-filled response was to declare: What else could they say and still defend the way things were done in ministry? This better response came a couple of years after hell left. Not all change is instant.

Later on, I realized something else: maybe they *were* right. Kinda.

I did have two crazy times. One of them might have actually been real and the other, absolutely not.

The first crazy happened before The Awakening.* I can firmly attest to the fact that something in the spirit realm was taking over me and it wasn't the Holy Spirit. I had no idea what was happening; my ability to function as a normal human being was diminishing and nobody had the right solution outside of the Blame Game and/or my need for strong medication. I wasn't playing that game and I wasn't taking that pill.

My fight to overcome the takeover, using Scripture, had begun.

* (To be described shortly. Huh-uh, no peeking ahead!)

Toilet Training

My battle against insanity began in 2002. If you were to use the bathroom in my house then, you would have been showered with Scripture. It was not my intention to save the world; at this point in my life, I was the one who needed rescuing. I taped empowering Scripture verses where I would be forced to see and read them, and that included next to the toilet—one of the few places where I was able to be still. Truth is, I was doing everything humanly possible to keep from going over the edge. I wasn't even certain where that edge existed or what was on the other side of it that I was trying desperately not to fall into. I just knew it had something to do with hell and I knew the devil wasn't fond of the Word of God, which is why I went around taping Scripture verses all over the house.

The world and the church were telling me I was on the verge of a nervous breakdown. The Lord was showing me that I was on the verge of a breakthrough.

During that same time period, I was given a CD of the written Word spoken over and over again, which might sound a tad boring, except that it was interspersed with song and jammed with an anointing. I played it repeatedly every day, speaking aloud alongside the woman whose voice spoke the Word, believing its power would crush my enemy.

And since the book was highly in vogue at that time, I resolved to pray *The Prayer of Jabez* daily, believing it sounded safe enough. I had no idea then what I was really saying nor that the "enlarge my territory" part would soon become my albatross.

The combination of these three actions was explosive and the power behind it was not my own. I had just mixed a lethal cocktail and the enemy had no choice but to drink, choke, and die.

Unfortunately, the devil resolved to take me with him and, for a brief period of time, I was able to glimpse what exactly WAS waiting for me on the other side of that edge.

I was right; it *was* hell.

It was right after seeing a vision of hell that a lady came into my kitchen and opened up the way to see heaven.

Chapter Five

The Awakening

Suddenly

I called her "the lady in the kitchen," because I didn't want anyone to know who it was that came to me that day—May 16, 2003, not that I remember it perfectly.... She told me just one thing that set me free in an instant. I suppose it was one of those "suddenlies" I had read about in Scripture. You can't psyche yourself up for a suddenly or put it on your calendar. They not only come unannounced, but they almost always come at around 11:59.

It was a pajama day and I was at the very edge of a nervous breakdown. It was nearly noon, so I suppose it WAS 11:59. She came to my door, and seeing her unnerved me; she rarely came to my house. She was one of the "rebellious" women in the church, the one whose husband was removed from the eldership because of her unruly nature. So she became "the lady in the kitchen" because the source, I had been told, was important to consider, and I didn't want to tell anyone that God had used *her* to set me free. According to them, He only uses the "called" and the "qualified."

The "lady in the kitchen" used to be my roommate, right about the time I got engaged. We were polar opposite in personality, but we bounced gently off each other with our differences. I think what I learned from her then that has stayed with me, even to this day, is how to keep a house clean and tidy. It was pre-pastor's wife training, I suppose.

Over the years, our relationship cooled as we became separated by our new responsibilities. She married and had four children in a row; while I married, struggled with infertility and wished I'd had her loins. When our paths did cross, it was usually about her frustration with the direction the church was going. After a while, she rarely spoke to me directly but I got wind of her complaints, usually through a common friend. I was, after all, the senior pastor's wife now and I suppose that put me on an unapproachable plane. I'm sure it did make me unreachable; I had fallen into the entitlement trap and it had me by the tongue. My ears, on the other hand, picked up all the buzz.

She wasn't the only one who questioned the decision-making in the church. I also suppose, with hindsight, some of her concerns were genuine, but some of them to me were unfounded. There were astounding manifestations of the power of God in our Women's Advances but she always seemed to find fault with the experiences. I knew them to be genuine and real and often wondered why she held back. She seemed frightened by something I didn't fully understand back then. I felt it best to just avoid her, for the most part, and let her husband deal with it. We did that a lot.

After her husband became an elder, she had access to a lot more of the details of the inner workings of the church leadership, so then her complaints became more on target, but I was warned to stay clear of her and that was easy enough to do. I was now the proud and happy mother of a newly adopted baby girl and had enough to occupy my time and thoughts.

The church had grown tremendously and the multiple visitors who came to our home to preach in our church were taking up all of my time. I put our relationship on the back burner and never thought much about her until her husband was asked to step down as an elder. Apparently, her tongue had gotten the best of her, she was quickly labeled a Jezebel (our overgrown phrase of the decade), and I just went along with it because I only knew her complaints to be rather harsh. She actually did have something worthwhile, maybe even invaluable, to say to us, but she lacked the grace to say it with discretion and we lacked the discretion to hear it with grace.

I peeked at her through the kitchen window and debated the idea of even answering the doorbell. Surely anything that brought *her* to my home could not be "of the Lord."

Through the half opened door, she said she wanted to tell me something, and that she believed the Lord had sent her. She said she was aware of something very bad going on inside me and maybe she could help. I don't remember anything about how she said this or what her face was saying, except that she seemed firm about it and I didn't know how to be mean.

And I was desperate.

I invited her into my kitchen and we sat down at the table. She spoke first, looking directly at me, as I cried into my hands, wishing I could disappear and wondering if this dark place I was in was taking me somewhere worse than where the Prozac I stopped taking only two weeks ago had taken me.

She only spoke four words to me and from that day on, I was never the same.

"It's NOT your fault."

"NO!" I remember crying out, "NONONO!" I put my hands up over my head as if to shield my mind. Something was making an entrance into my thought life—something that was falling from the heavens that I was terrified to receive even though it was working far better and far faster than any pill.

"The guilt and condemnation that's been put on you is not from God," she continued.

I told her to stop saying that, that it was too good to be true. I so badly wanted to believe what she was telling me, but I couldn't. I didn't want to receive something so wonderful only to have it torn away from me again, making the wound in my heart deeper and more painful. So I continued to raise my hands yelling, "NONONO!"

But then something happened, something that made my hands turn just slightly from a defensive position into a welcoming pose, something like worship.

It became worship.

All those shackles I'd heard about, but didn't know entombed me, fell off.

—Suddenly, completely, and to my utter delight.

I was carrying guilt and condemnation around that was not mine to bear, that had already been taken to the Cross, but I had embraced as my own. It was a finished work and I had been allowing it to finish me. And now it was gone. Suddenly gone. Every ounce of oppression and depression and great darkness.

I wasn't on the verge of a breakdown—I was on the verge of a breakthrough.

Awake My Soul

My born-again experience was a Saul/Paul conversion. It was loud and in-your-face and over-the-top. This new thing from the lady in the kitchen was similar. It wasn't quite as loud, but it was a drastic, over-the-top change. I didn't know what to call what had just happened to me, but in time it came to be known as The Awakening. There's no other way to describe it. I had been about to lose my sanity over something called legalism and in one of the Lord's infamous "suddenlies," I became a new person. Again.

The Awakening occurred exactly 30 years, 3 weeks and 3 days after I was born-again. Hmmm... And just like my original conversion, the oppression was lifted, the confusion transformed into order, the darkness left the room known as my mind, and I was as high as a kite.

I absolutely do not remember anything that happened the rest of that day. What I do remember is what happened the next day.

I woke up about two hours earlier than my normal time and went right to the Word with a notebook and pen in hand and eyes wide open. It became my new best habit and to this day, it has continued to be my normal day's routine. (Okay, to be honest, Facebook recently interrupted that early morning time for a season, but I have gotten back on track.)

I had no idea that guilt and condemnation weighed so much. I had no idea that talking to God was not one-sided. I had no idea what He was about to show me next.

That very first week following The Awakening, I was led to the story of the Good Samaritan. Two religious men walked past a half-dead man laying on a road that went from Jerusalem to Jericho. Neither one did a thing to help the wounded man; it was a Samaritan who finally came to his aid.

The road between Jerusalem and Jericho was beset with thieves and you were pretty much taking your life into your hands by traveling it. Why the man was on the road in the first place, we might never know. Was it imperative he travel that route to get to his destination, or was he merely flippant about the dangers of the journey? Or could he have been one of the thieves himself? The Bible doesn't tell us because it doesn't matter. What matters is that the man is half-dead and cannot heal himself and that fact appears obvious to anyone who saw him.

When we make a judgment about who deserves what, or why someone is wounded in the first place, we begin to accuse and condemn and that's legalism territory.

It is always devoid of grace.

The religious guys were traveling the same route themselves. What was that about? See what I mean?

Still, as I was reading this passage, I began to see myself in the half-dead man and thought the lady in the kitchen just might have been my Good Samaritan. Samaritans were not very popular with the religious community.

"Who do these two religious men remind you of?" asked the Lord. I hesitated but had to admit they were a lot like my husband and my pastor (the pastor who was next to my husband in seniority and who was assigned to be my own pastor). When I told them how much I was hurting, they seemed, in that same

sense, to walk right past me. Oh, but they did *say* something, something like, *"It's your fault you're like this,"* and *"If you really loved the Lord..."* and the overdone and highly irritating, *"Take drugs."*

Was this the Lord? Was He telling me that these two men, the men I loved most in all the world, also had that same critical spirit? Had they made a false judgment about me in the same way the priest and Levite appeared to have done? Had they also condemned me in the same way, choosing that I suffer the consequences of what they deemed to be my sin?

The lady in the kitchen had said, "The guilt and condemnation is not from God," and with that word, I felt all the oppression melt away.

Is that what You meant, Lord?

I hadn't finished reading the rest of the story when I sensed His Spirit, hovering above, around and within me, giving me insight and understanding about something I wasn't even searching for and didn't know I needed to hear. It all came down to this one story and it all came rushing at me in one giant revelation. For the first time in a long time, my heart was hearing His voice, reassuring me in the kindest way that this revelation was indeed from Him. I found myself rethinking and questioning the whole reason for the Cross.

All these years, I was fully immersed in what I thought was God and suddenly I knew it wasn't God at all: it was religion, in one sense, but not at all pure and most certainly defiled.*

I was on the threshold of an awakening that would introduce me, again, to my Savior. I was entering into a new walk with the

Lord and I would be able to see Him as He was, and not how someone interpreted Him to be.

And, I was about to discover grace again.

Or, maybe even, for the very first time.

* James 1:27 (NRSV) *Religion that is pure and undefiled before God, the Father, is this: to care for orphans and widows in their distress, and to keep oneself unstained by the world.*

Over The Top

I was so high in the Spirit I would have to define myself as being as drunk as the people in the second chapter of Acts. I make no apologies for the high I was on or the way I acted. Deliverance from death should resonate out of every pore. Did Mary and Martha scream aloud when their brother came back to life? I would think so. I would hope so.

Jesus asked the people around Lazarus to unwrap the bindings that encircled his body. The lady in the kitchen was asked to unwrap the ones that circled my mind. You are, at the very least, supposed to throw a party over things like that.

But no one threw anything, except maybe they threw me—under the bus. The elders and the pastors and my daughter and my husband saw that something happened to me but they were unable to see that what was released from me still entombed them.

So, yes, now I did for sure appear crazy and it was crazy wonderful.

2 Cor. 5:7*

I had never really lost my faith. I had just misplaced it.

I knew it was somewhere in the "house" and I had to think long and hard about where I last had it and what I might have done with it without thinking.

I wasted a lot of time searching in vain.

I had it all along, on top of my head and right next to my missing glasses.

For a time, I couldn't see well and everything was blurry; but then I put them both back where they belonged and things cleared up a lot.

*2 COR. 5:7 (KJV) *For we walk by faith, not by sight.*

The Ladies Room

I heard about the Tuesday morning women's meeting long before I ever attended it. When someone in leadership says, *"No you can't go,"* you want to believe you are being protected somehow against something that would be *harmful* to your spirit. The idea that it might actually *free* your spirit was never intimated, so I stayed clear of the meetings. I was given this warning: *"It was started by a rebellious woman and has no church backing. No man is involved with it and because women can get off track without pastoral guidance, it can get into cult-like activity."*

Well, gee, I sure wouldn't want to be a part of anything like that. At least, not until I needed to and not until the Lord told me it wasn't what they said it was, rather it was actually a good place for me to go.

Sometime during the 1980's, a woman from the area, known for her radical thinking, invited some of her lady friends over to study the Bible. Period. The group was eventually picked up by another woman with a bigger living room but the same hungry crew. It evolved from a need for fellowship into something far greater. It became the breaking ground for healthy soil to form, for seeds to be planted, for women to blossom and the Spirit of God to move. The Spirit was given top priority, which is probably why there's such nice fruit growing off its vine all these many years.

The first time I went to one of their meetings, it was because I knew instinctively the Lord was prompting me to go. It was right after the Awakening. I rang the bell at the door; when you go to someone's house for the first time, you do that. The next time, I was instructed, you walk right in. The woman who answered the door was familiar with my background and shared with me later that she felt like Rhoda answering the door and finding Peter standing there.

Apparently, both Peter and I had been brought out of prison and knew exactly where to go next for some good fellowship.

Jealousy

Out of nowhere, the Lord spoke to me.

Okay, so it's never really out of nowhere from His end. But it's always out of nowhere from within me. It's usually when I stop thinking for one split second and He manages to squeeze a sentence into the rush of other things taking up my thought space. Yeah, I know. It happens a lot in the bathroom.

Anyway, it wasn't in the bathroom. It was at the kitchen sink. I was standing at the sink and looking out the window into the back yard and I heard Him clearly say, *"Your husband is jealous of us."*

The rush of other things were quickly replaced by new thoughts. *Jealous.* I was having such a wonderful time rediscovering the Lord and enjoying the liberty that happens when guilt and condemnation are no longer binding up who you are as a person. Jealous is a funny word for how my husband would respond to what was happening to me. Shouldn't he be happy for me? Shouldn't he rejoice with me? But all I had been detecting was detachment. It was not what I wanted or expected from him.

The very next day, my husband came to me and said, and yes, these were his exact words, because I wrote them down in disbelief:

"I'm actually jealous of the relationship you're having with God right now and can't figure out why He would bless someone as evil as you are with His presence."

Es-Courting

Following my suddenly, I began to journal every day, communing with the Lord every morning at the breakfast table became a regular part of my waking hours, usually between 6 and 7 in the morning. The Bible finally had something to say! I began to experience powerful revelations about who God really was and what it was that kept me from really knowing Him. Every revelation was saturated with the love of the Lord. I called it Java with Jehovah in the Tent of Meeting. I read that somewhere, so I stole it.

It was something more than just a devotional time. It was HIS devotion to me—revealing truths as only HE can—gently and firmly and supernaturally. If He tells me He is the truth, He is telling me about His nature, His character, His essence. He told me, much to my chagrin, that I was in an unhealthy church environment and an unhealthy marriage and I put my hands to my ears and said *lalalalala* and begged Him to change everything around me so that I could stay—stay at my church, stay in this marriage, and stay in this house and just wait for everything to change around me. Then it would all be happily-ever-after again. I was, after all, a pastor's wife in a born-again, spirit-filled church—had been for nearly three decades—and I loved the calling right up to this moment and wanted it to continue.

Except that nothing around me was changing. I had to watch my family and my friends and my church and my world be pulled away so that I could heal and I could change. I did not understand it at the time and it took years for me to understand this was an act of love.

So while the great divide took place, somebody had to be at fault and the choice was unanimous. I was new to all this communing with God and came across to many as finally having gone over the edge. I was labeled insane and as long as I was labeled, I was, I thought, doomed for life.

There was nothing brave in me that had the stamina to walk willingly away from what and who I loved. There was nothing martyr-like about my character that I was offering to the Lord in the same silent fashion as Mary's ponderings. There was no strength within my own self that enabled me to stand in the truth of what was being revealed to me, morning after morning at my breakfast table.

But He made it nearly impossible for me to go back, or backwards, and while my feet sometimes dragged as He drew me to Himself, I had no choice but to trust the Lord to remove me from where I would not grow and take me to a place where the healing could begin.

For a very long time, my heart did not follow my feet, so He just wooed me for a while till my heart caught up.

Do You Love Me?

I was not at all happy with the idea that God would allow me to live in deception for such a long time. I had assumed I was following Him as best I knew how and had expected Him to take me into the Land of His-Perfect-Will-For-My-Life. At the time, I made absolutely no connection between my walk

with God and the mass of Israelites dragging out a road trip that should have taken days and not years. I continued to look at the same side of the same mountain before I realized I had nailed my foot to the floor and was traveling around in circles.

My real struggle was not so much believing God was opening my eyes of understanding, but discovering I had lived over three decades in a place of ignorance. I had come to learn about the Sadducees and Pharisees and knew without question that Jesus was talking about Jewish Rabbis, Catholic priests and Presbyterian ministers. Now everything the Lord was opening up to me was confirming that I was *one of them*, that I had spent the better part of my life serving God in a church atmosphere that mirrored those Pharisees I'd so easily judged, the very ones Jesus was constantly rebuking.

"Do you love me?" Jesus asks.

Peter, the *Everyman* of the New Testament, pretty much screwed up his response. He had to hear the question three times and never really understood the implication. It grieved Peter to think that *"Yes, Lord,"* was insufficient.

What did Jesus want to hear from Peter that Peter didn't grasp?

"You know all things," Peter tells him. *"You know that I love you."*

I can hear Peter making a mental list of all the good things he had done since he joined the inner circle. It took a death and resurrection to begin the understanding process.

The same thing happened to Much-Afraid in *Hinds' Feet on High Places.** The Great Shepherd asks her:

"*Do you love me enough to trust me...even if everything in the wide world seemed to say that I was deceiving you...all along?*

"*Would it be that she could never trust...Him again...to know that she had been deceived by one she was certain could not deceive?*

"*Much-Afraid looks directly into his face: '...if you can deceive me, you may...I must love you as long as I continue to exist. I cannot live without loving you.'*"

He has asked me the same question and more than once. Like Peter, I mentally list my attributes.

Come on, God. I've got history with You.

I poured out my life for You.

I was the pastor's wife and I counseled the flock and cleaned church toilets and entertained Godly people in my home. I stayed faithful to my husband and went to all the services and took notes at Bible Studies. I did the nursery gig and even taught junior church, which You personally know I hated but no one else would do it. For decades, I changed diapers on babies who are now married with children. I said the sinner's prayer and meant it. Why would You allow me to stay ignorant for so long?

My answer has to be the same one Much-Afraid gave the great Shepherd:

"*Of course I love you; even if I, too, have been allowed to live in deception. I cannot live without loving you.*"

* *Hinds' Feet on High Places* by Hannah Hurnard, first published in 1955, republished by many different companies today

Grace

I met her at that prayer meeting, Bible study thingy I mentioned before that meets on a Tuesday morning. When I was first introduced to Grace, she looked at me with the eyes of a Prophetess, because she was. A prophetess. I didn't know it at the time though because I didn't know prophetesses even existed, but I knew she saw something in me that I couldn't yet see.

You have to understand one thing about shock and post traumatic stress disorder, which I was told later by professionals that my losses had brought on. You don't know you're in it and you don't know you have it. So you look like the about-to-become-venison deer in the headlights but there is no light on at all. It is a horrible place to visit when you have no recollection of even traveling anywhere. You just know you're somewhere you have never been and that you are lost and at the same time pretending as much as you can that everything is all right and there is nothing wrong with you, God forbid. But God doesn't always forbid it because we are, after all, still living in these human bodies and we have to go through something called *process* before we can, well, *process* what it is we have just gone through. I suppose that works for spiritual trips through the desert, too.

So back to Grace. I think she saw that the lights were out and wanted to know who flipped the switch and why. She befriended me. She talked to me. She took me to lunch. She saw my hurt and looked past the vacancy sign. And then one day, and I'm sure she doesn't even remember this, she simply looked at me across a dinner table and said, "I love you, Carol."

The next day, I wrote what she said in my journal and asked the Lord how that could be because I was so evil and demonic and rebellious and a hypocrite. That is what my husband had been telling me for years. I guess ministers use religious terminology to replace the words that get bleeped out on television. So if I was evil and now I was meeting a Godly, Christian woman who told me I was **not** evil, but indeed lovable, how can that happen? I was conflicted. *How could she*, I wrote down in my journal, *possibly love someone who was so evil?*

The journal entries continued for several months as I continued to wait for an answer to my identity dilemma. This was something that took years to unfold because I had yet to go through a process that would show me who I was.

Several days later, I came into my office and saw my husband's hairbrush sitting on my desk. I was never able to make the connection, until months later, that he had left it there by mistake after I left the house, while he secretly read my journal entries and my e-mails. And made photocopies and printouts of them. And gave them out like candy to interested parties, like other ministers and our teen-age daughter.

"This is what husbands do," he told our daughter, "When their wives are acting wacky. They read their journals."

What I had written about Grace was used as fodder.

"See?" My husband wrote me in an e-mail months after our separation. "Even **you** know you are evil."

My husband was lying to me about who I was.
Sad that he did that. Sadder that I believed it was true.
I don't believe it anymore, thank God.

Still, it took a long time for me to, well, *process* that—to *process* the truth that I am not an evil woman at all, but a virtuous one, and in His sight, quite a beauty.

Still A Small Voice

Sometimes, when you are *doing* nothing important, God comes in and *says* something important. I was just walking down the hall in my house and I heard Him. I'm talking about *audibly* heard Him.

It was only the second time I heard His voice this way. I would hear it again years later, when I needed to.

What I heard was unnerving and made no sense to me at the time.

"I have called you to be a Prophetess."

Okay, Carol, maybe they ARE right. Maybe you have lost it entirely. Except that it was His voice and I knew it and my second response, after being unnerved, was

"What is a prophetess?"

In our church, at least at that time, there were only prophets. Women were not in ministry so the *ess* at the end had no bearing. There was no place for them in the New Testament. (Philip's four daughters were ignored.) I thought I had read something about a prophetess in a book someone gave me and began to search the house. We collected books like hoarders and I had a lot to rummage through, but was unable to find it. So I asked Him to find it for me. I felt that book had an answer to my question. If

I'm called to do something, it only makes sense to know what it is I should be doing. A no-brainer.

The next day, I found the book in the drawer of my make-up table, a place I go to every morning so people who see me will not think I have the flu. There was no reason for it to be there. It was never there before.

I had never needed it before.

A Smaller Voice, Still

What I learned about a prophetess was not a pleasant read. She is a female prophet and usually what she has to say about a matter brings on a similar response met by most of the prophets from the Old and New Testaments. They are laughed at, attacked, and destroyed. In today's more sophisticated society, weapons of steel and stone are replaced by words of mockery. It is easier to ridicule the bearer of the news than to actually receive it. That is what I did, exactly, to the lady in the kitchen.

Especially unhappy with whatever the prophetess's voice carries, are her husband and her pastor and when they are one and the same person, the word she carries becomes the focus of an all-out assault.

I told an elder what the Lord told me. It was a huge mistake. It only caused me more trouble. It gave the elders and my husband another weapon to use against me. It was the last piece of hard evidence they needed to prove their diagnosis that I was indeed crazy.

A prophetess must learn how to find God's voice in the midst of all the others, discern the timing and the right pair of ears that need to hear the message, and say whatever it is God said. That's the easy part. The hard part is letting it go, enduring what is bound to be a backlash and a whole lot of rejection, and biting her tongue, a tongue that wants very much to add an apology at the end.

In other words, she has to fight against everything that defines her as a woman.

I began to pray for the gift of hospitality.

Section Three

Break Down

"To everything there is a season...a time to break down..." Ecclesiastes 3:1a, 3b

Chapter Six
The Bus crash

Projectile Vomiting

My husband and I were eating our lunch in stone silence. That we were even eating at the same table at the same time was unusual. The news-at-noon provided us with background sounds. Once a week, the news station would have a guest psychologist discuss whatever term or trauma was popular at the time. The Lord told me to pay attention to the discussion of the day.

The female psychologist was explaining the term "Projection," clarifying to the audience that this is what someone does to another person when they are feeling guilty about something themselves. It's the transference of that guilt. The guilty party can't carry the burden of their particular transgression. They have to get rid of it, so they accuse someone else of the same thing.

Later that day, I looked up the word *projection* in the dictionary and read the definition: *PSYCHOLOGY: the unconscious ascription of a personal thought, feeling, or impulse, especially one considered undesirable, to somebody else.* Those dictionaries are ever so careful not to use the "sin" word in describing something *undesirable*, unless, of course, they're defining sin itself. I was willing to settle for *undesirable*, but wanted something a little more secure. I wanted the Word.

"So, okay, Lord, he's probably projecting something on me, but what is that all about and where is it in Scripture?"

Later that week, I found myself studying the book of Leviticus, not one of my personal favorites and certainly not one I would want to memorize. Chapter 16 tells the story of Aaron and the two-goat sacrifice. Aaron slaughtered the first goat as

a sin offering, sprinkling its blood on the Mercy Seat. This was where the forgiveness part happened. He then laid his hands on the head of the second goat and spoke the sins, iniquities, and transgressions of the people on it and sent it into the wilderness, where the guilt part was dealt with. Goats have a short shelf-life in the wilderness—like, one day.

"This is the reason you're having a lot of your mental issues," Father told me. *"You can't carry someone else's sin for them. It's not your fault and it's not your responsibility. Don't allow that to be done to you. He's not fighting you, he's fighting Me and he can't face his own issues, so he's trying to make them YOUR issues. Don't allow him to do that."*

It explained a lot about my head issues.

It also explained a lot about my husband. As he continued to resolve to do scape-goating, I resolved to get well. This headed us in two separate directions and that is, sadly, where each of us went.

Again, Microsoft Word 7 on my computer isn't recognizing "scapegoating" as a word, but I am positive it is an active verb and I have the head trauma to prove it.

Juxtaposed Journaling

Early on in my journaling venture, I struggled with being honest with my own self and our marriage. It became a painful time, writing down what I was feeling into a spiral ring notebook and trying to balance these thoughts with all the training I had been given about submission. The mere act of writing it down, I was convinced, was an act of rebellion to authority, making it easy to understand why I was considered rebellious or labeled the ever-infamous name, Jezebel. In reality, I was so afraid to hurt the Lord. I wasn't so much afraid *of* Him. I loved Him. But I was afraid I was sinning *against* Him with my written-down thoughts.

These two journal entries, exactly as they are written here, juxtapose each other in irony, in reality and in hind-sight. The first one actually occurred just months prior to The Awakening. My journaling attempts were sporadic at best.

12/28/02 – (My husband) is a stubborn, controlling man and I am fearful that I will choose not to be with him anymore. This is what I plainly see: a father to a daughter (from his first marriage) *whom he has never accepted on the basis of who she is but on what she is not (which is Christian). He pushes the Lord on her and I see why she pulls back – he is not loving her unconditionally. With me, it is as if I have to earn his love. He denies this completely. It is this spirit of deception that blinds him to this truth. And so, as long as he denies hearing truth, he will live with a lie, and I will live with a constant battle. This is what I'm having a hard time doing.*

3/26/12 - My husband, to his credit, wasn't always stubborn and controlling and arrogant. He was kind on so many levels and you don't live with someone nearly three decades and allow them to beat you up. Or maybe you do. Maybe you just don't realize you're being "beaten"* until the "bruises" begin to show and other people see them and, you hope, are kind enough to tell you you're both black and blue and bleeding profusely.

115

But no one came and no one told me except for the "suddenly" lady, at least not until after the divorce.

I bled out for a few painful years, but I healed. I healed.

* (My husband never physically beat me, only verbally and emotionally.)

More Journaling

Here are a few more tidbits from my journal entries that I wrote down during that time.

"Power in the pulpit doesn't point to perfection in the home." (My husband was and is a very good preacher. Multitudes of people have been led to the Lord, lives have been changed, and diseases have been healed. He helped so many, while at the same time hurting me and others.)

"Hot on the altar, cold in the bedroom."

"It's quite possible I am not unlike the one sheep Jesus left the 99 to rescue, except I thought it was because I was lost. It never crossed my mind that it might be because I was black."

"So what is submission and what is stupidity and what is sin?"

"Some prayer needs to come out of the closet."

"I believe if we gain an ounce of religiosity, we lose a pound of Jesus."

" 'I'm sorry, Lord. While I appreciate that you have done wonderful things for me as I have walked through this wilderness, I would never wish or want to walk this way again.'

"To which He replied, *I would go to the Cross again.*'

Ouch..."

" 'What's so different about us Christians?' you ask. We're sinners and our life was hugely interrupted with forgiveness and mercy. We ride on grace all the way through to the end."

The Crazed Sinner

<u>Here is a list of some of the crazy behaviors I exhibited while serving as a pastor's wife:</u>

I changed the furniture around too many times.

I was never satisfied no matter what house we lived in and I always wanted to move.

I got crude sometimes when I talked.

I interrupted people when they were talking.

I talked and laughed too much and too loud.

I was careless with finances, shopping too often.

I behaved selfishly from time to time.

I sought compliments and was proud.

I gave in to PMS.

I had panic attacks over the years.

I was afraid to travel—in a car as well as on a plane—which sadly prevented me from joining my husband on many of his overseas trips or when he was asked to lead seminars in various churches throughout the country.

This is what the Lord told me to do about it when I presented them to Him:

"Come to me all you who are weary and heavy laden and I will give you rest" (Matthew 11:28 NASB).

Here is a list of the sins I committed that no one brought to my attention:

I judged my church family's dilemmas with my flesh; I focused in on their flaws, when my real "job" was to remind my Christian friends of His love and faithfulness and encourage them in and through their struggles.

Here is a list of all the other sins God has thrown in my face:

(Actually, I started to list all my sins into my journal one morning, so I could approach my problems head-on—my idea—and I heard Him say, clear as a crystal bell, "I don't remember them; why should YOU? That's what got you into trouble in the first place!")

Disconnect

I overheard my husband say something very unpleasant and degrading. He said it about a family member. He had hoped the man's daughter would get pregnant out of wedlock so he would stop bragging about his attractive, intelligent, and successful children. He said it to our daughter who, at the time, was a teenager. I told him later, when we were alone, that I'd overheard him and that I not only did not like what I heard him say, he had pronounced a curse and had said it to our daughter.

I could tell that he agreed it was the wrong thing to do. He replied, "Even if you're right, I won't listen to anything you say because it's coming out of your mouth."

It was at that moment, and not the moment it was legal on paper, that I saw my marriage might be coming to an end.

No Accident

My husband answered the phone and from my end, I only heard what he was saying, "That couldn't happen. I've been praying for you."

It was early in the evening when our daughter called to say she was in another car accident, her third one in three months. None of them, we later learned, were her fault.

The next morning, I opened the Word and randomly found myself in I Peter 3:7.

119

"Husbands, likewise, dwell with them with understanding, giving honor to the wife, as to the weaker vessel, and as being heirs together of the grace of life, that your prayers may not be hindered."

Retirement

The official reason for my husband no longer being a part of the leadership at my old church was listed as "Retirement." He was actually *forced* into early retirement. He was supposed to leave looking good. He did and he didn't. He left but he didn't look good. Word got out that other things were going on behind the scenes but nobody with pulpit access was talking about what those other things really were, which was a reoccurring theme and makes complete sense if you are image-conscious.

What I am about to say here comes with a disclaimer. What I tell you was going on *behind* the scenes might not actually be what happened because I was kept in the dark the whole time. I had to make assumptions. Yes, I know. But no one was talking to me at home and no one, outside of the mole (which you will learn about shortly), was talking to me in church. Anything I did learn was via the telephone through an appointed "talking head," a minister "hired" as my official pastor. It was his job to keep me in the loop about what was going on. His connection with me was as short-lived as everyone else in my life was about to become.

During this time, I found a copy of an e-mail I wasn't supposed to see. It was written to my pastor by a well-known man of God, telling him to force my husband into early retirement rather than fire him. It said my husband would probably divorce me soon after that and they were to let me go to fend for myself. I was not their problem.

I tried to find the Scriptural basis for this, but apparently it doesn't exist.

I don't think anybody in leadership really understood what was going on. No one in my circle had ever gone through anything like this before and no one knew how to handle it. I learned they sought outside help, and thus this e-mail ensued.

I assumed the actual process of pushing me out of fellowship was already set in place. It was easy to do and just as easy to detect—don't talk to Carol. They did a great job ignoring me, and so I began to make those assumptions. One lady from church, married to an elder, started to have a conversation with me about some things that were going on and right in the middle of a sentence said, "Oh, I can't talk to you about this. You're not in leadership anymore." That conversation occurred the day after an elders and wives meeting, the one my husband and I didn't get invited to. We were slowly but surely being ripped out of both fellowship and relationship.

I assumed most everyone in leadership knew prior to my husband's "retirement" that a divorce was soon to follow. He had taken out a separate savings account in another bank and while I knew about it, it went right over my head. Pastors won't divorce their wives, I thought, so it meant nothing to me. Apparently this knowledge, and a lot more no one ever shared with me, made it easier for them to dispose of both of us first and then whatever happened after that would have no connection to the church.

Again, this makes complete sense if you are image-conscious. I hated what they were doing, but I understood their thinking completely. I was still trying to rearrange my own brain and eliminate the old way of thinking. I had no Plan B outside of existing. And making assumptions.

That's why all this comes with a disclaimer. I was putting pieces of the puzzle together because something terrible was happening in the church and in our marriage and I needed to know what that meant for me. So I had to fend for myself.

I continued to make assumptions in my own home by listening. I listened to the Lord. I listened to the one-sided conversations my husband was having on the telephone. I overheard him talking to people in leadership and trying to get them to turn on the new senior pastor. He did not like the direction the church was heading in. It wasn't his vision and he was certain he had made a mistake when entrusting this man to assume his old job. He had no idea he himself was about to be booted out of the church.

I listened to my heart a lot, too. Hearts carry a lot of truth, especially when Jesus lives there.

I was in constant communication with the Lord on every level my desperation brought me to. I spent hours every day either in prayer, Bible study or just listening to a song by the Casting Crowns called *The Voice of Truth*, a song I played repeatedly. I was in constant battle, the whole time, as to whether I was really the world's worse sinner and everything I thought was the Lord was just another deception, or I was hearing the Voice Of Truth for myself.

At one point, I was forced to apologize and confess to the elders that I was not hearing from the Lord. I did so out of fear and ignorance. I did so out of survival mode.

I've been wanting to take that back. I know now why people will confess to something they never did if they are interrogated and berated enough to want to get the whole ordeal over with. Surrender to a lie is often more appealing than the battle to stand firm in the truth.

Half of me was saying, "If you don't stand up to evil, it will walk all over you." The other half was wondering if maybe I really was Jezebel's twin sister. I was confused about whether I was a sinner saved by grace or a child of the King. And while I wrapped myself in that contradiction for years, I continued to assume.

I found it ironic to overhear someone comment about how hard it would be for me to not be the pastor's wife anymore. Not being the senior pastor's wife anymore was easy. No longer being a wife, period, was a lot worse. But not to be a mom or a longtime friend, or an only sister anymore—those losses were the worst of the worst.

I had forgotten some of the details concerning rejection and false accusations leading up to the crucifixion. I had forgotten the part of Scripture that speaks of sharing in His suffering. I had forgotten that sometimes there is pain involved when you decide to obey. I was about to be reminded.

Prophetic Insight

It was such a strange thing to watch and hear. We were seated in the church on a Saturday morning, all the elders and their wives and three visiting prophetic ministers from out of the immediate area. It was one of the last leadership meetings we would both be invited to attend.

We had a service the night before where these men used their prophetic gifts and had what we referred to as a Presbytery Meeting. Prophetic men were used to encourage certain pre-chosen members of the church with words they received directly from the Lord. I didn't have a problem with it then and I don't have a problem with it now. I do know without a doubt Who is behind this ministry and am continually encouraged in my faith when I see the prophetic word in action like that.

I can't recall who the three men were, save one lone man. He seemed broken, or battle-weary or perhaps both. He struggled his way through the evening and I saw clearly that the words he spoke were truth, that he was right on with what he perceived, but there were problems with the vessel. He seemed terribly fragile.

We asked these men to address the group of elders and wives the next day. I have no idea what they were told about any of us before the meeting. I trusted we would do what we'd always done—keep quiet about what was happening in the church and allow the gift to reveal itself. It was hoped we would glean from their expertise as each one walked to the front of the church and shared whatever was burdening their heart in regards to the church and its leadership. When it came time for the broken vessel to speak, he let us know he had nothing to bring to the table but this one thought: the leadership needed to start behaving a little bit more like me.

He said the group needed to adopt a spirit of acceptance and stop zeroing in on the faults in other people. He also spoke of my own personal need to receive because I had been giving long enough.

I told you it was a strange thing to watch and hear. I wanted to hide. I wanted to sing. I wanted to say YES, YES, YES. But that's not what I did. I just sat there, stunned. Because a short time prior, the "suddenly" lady had come into my kitchen and spoken the words that set me on this new path, and Grace had told me she loved me, and now this man I only met one time, the night before, was saying the strangest thing. And he was saying it to a group of people who knew more about me than they were letting on. They knew I was about to be divorced and they believed I was mentally ill.

They were partly right. I would go on to be divorced but there was no way I was going to embrace the mental illness part. I knew that I knew that I knew I was on the way to soundness of mind. I just hadn't yet been enlightened about what it really was that was binding up my soul and polluting my mind. But somehow this prophetic man did.

He went on to tell the elders and their wives they needed to lighten up and not make so many judgments. He told them not to be so stiff and uptight. He told them they needed to be accepting and welcoming like I was, so that there would be healing in that act of acceptance for hurting people. He said

it all in a really nice way and I enjoyed it in a really nice way. He told me directly, and in front of them, not to let this word overwhelm me or make me think I had to do anything about fixing the situation myself or make me carry any kind of false burden or responsibility.

I was called into the office a few days later for another one of those dreaded confrontations, this time with the new pastor. Nothing was mentioned about what this man had said to the group about me, but I was told it was true that I needed to receive something and that something was most certainly some intense counseling.

Head Call

Over the years, I received many prophetic words about what the Lord wanted to do with my life. Some were spoken through women, which I often suspected brought an immediate cancellation or questioning to much of whatever was said. Most of the time, I have to admit, I was encouraged in these words, but always and only up to a point—the point where it became obvious to the leadership that maybe some of the things spoken over me, or over others in our church, were too far-reaching.

This is hard to believe, but certain people in leadership felt there were occasions when someone being prayed for internally manipulated the prophet through demonic means by willing them to say what they wanted to hear. We were so gullible, we actually swallowed this. Combine that with their pre-determined-by-the-leadership spiritual immaturity, flawed heart condition, and misinterpretation of what was said, and you've got complete mind control and a perfect roadmap to confusion! It robbed people of receiving a personal gift from God! And it inevitably annihilated anyone's vision and the confirmation they were seeking for that vision.

Up to a point, I understood what they were saying. You don't put a power saw into the hands of a two-year-old and tell the child to build a house. There is always a space of time between the word that is spoken and the culmination of that word. The emphasis, however, often seemed to be on one's worthiness to receive a blessing; we seemed to lack knowing how to encourage or stir up the calling or the gifts that came with it. I could sense there were a lot of judgment calls being made and not enough discerning going on. Simply put, our imperfections were used against us and that, at times, became the criteria for determining if a prophetic word was or was not appropriate.

I can't speak for the others, but for me, it added to my deep, and by now inordinate, need for approval, and affirmation of many things I believed the Lord had spoken to my heart. I came into the Kingdom with a deep need and now it was growing deeper. It was unhealthy and I was fully aware of it.

Toward the end of my marriage, and just before my husband was forced into early retirement, he was being honored for his years of service and his new upgrade in the Kingdom—the calling of an apostle. He was given a formal service, a grand party, and many words of accolade by area ministers about all the wonderful things he had done as a pastor. I mentioned to

someone that I was right there with him all those twenty-five years of serving, and would have liked to have been honored or acknowledged in some way.

Once again, I was called into the office and heavily rebuked for saying that. Apparently the person I said it to felt it was wrong of me to even express my hurt and it needed to be reported to the new pastor. I went out from that meeting with my tail between my legs and pouted about the issue until my lower lip became one with the floor. I overplayed the whole thing in my head and believed I was entitled to at least some kind of recognition or a simple thank you. I gathered a pound of courage, went back to the church office a few days later, and confronted the pastor to find out the real reason why no one wanted to honor me. He told me I had a big head and it would get bigger if I were given any kind of public recognition.

My "big head" became immediately and substantially deflated.

Honest Attempts

There were three honest attempts made to salvage our marriage.

1) The church flew in a pastor and his wife from another state to counsel us. They allowed me to choose who would counsel us, so I chose the man who told me he thought my husband was weird. I was hoping he might address the basis for that.

2) My husband suggested we take ballroom dancing lessons. Doing something outside the confines of church might help rekindle our relationship.

3) Our daughter helped my husband buy presents for me for Christmas and birthdays and anniversaries and Valentine's Day that she thought I would like and that maybe might help us love one another again.

Every attempt only broke my heart a little bit more.

1) The couple who counseled us simply put a band-aid on the cancer. Apparently the pastor still remembered the encounter from three years earlier. I was told to continue to bear silently my burden of truth—yes, the one he had given me earlier—the one I really shouldn't have had to carry. I said I would try. He stayed far away from the issue I had hoped he would dig into.

2) The dance lessons only proved that cheek-to-cheek did not mean heart-to-heart.

3) I always knew the gifts reflected my daughter's desperate desire to heal our marriage. It was her hurt that mattered most, and I told my husband we should really try to work things out for the sake of our only child's broken heart. He laughed at me and called me a name.

Years later, I saw our divorce for what it really was: a rescue operation set in place by a jealous Lover.

The Lord told me He would take care of my daughter. He told me He loved her more than I did.

The Crash

It was a horrible accident.

Accident. No, I can't use that word. Nothing, if you truly walk with the Lord, is an accident.

So, I guess, it was a horrible on-purpose.

My husband and I were struggling to keep up appearances. That's what you do when you don't want anyone to know the truth, the behind-closed-doors thing. It's a slight-of-hand trick; it's bait-and-switch. It's all theater—you act, you perform; you fool the crowd. The longer they accept what they see, the longer life the story has, and so it continued to play out with the two of us for those few remaining months before the final separation. We gave it the whole fall season—a whole semester, while our daughter was away at college. Better said, I submitted to it for that long. But I guess I don't do "fake" too well.

It all began when my husband decided to house hunt with the intention of finding a place where we could keep up appearances and he could keep his "apostleship" position. We moved into a two-level house that accommodated one spouse on one floor and one spouse on the other. Each level had a bedroom, living area and full bath. We tried working things out as a couple by staying on the first floor, but it was short-lived. I remained upstairs while he moved into the remodeled basement and into what had been our daughter's room. Our daughter was away at Bible school in another state, so she wasn't around when all of this happened. He planned to return upstairs when she came home for Christmas vacation and continue the charade until she left again for the second semester.

I played along with the plan because I had no plan B to choose from...at least not yet.

From the outside, we looked like a couple.

Yeah. Rev. and Mrs. Gingerbread.

Nine Won One

There is a turning point—there always is—when you clearly alter your direction or your season or your life. I only know it happened one cold December night when something snapped in my husband's brain and he began to spew out all that he had held in for years. It was sparked by an honest attempt, on my part, to reconcile. Somehow, I found the courage to apologize to him for my failures and my weaknesses, hoping he would hear my heart. That's all I ever wanted from him, that he would hear my heart.

I rarely raised my voice; it brought too much fear into an already fearful confrontation. This night was no exception.

When the spewing began, it had no commas or periods but one long list after another of everything I ever said or did that sanctioned the right for him to define me as a demonic, evil woman. By then, the church had forced him into early retirement to avoid the ugly process of actually firing him, and his pay check

was cut by two-thirds. He was hiding (I later learned) a secret sin in his heart and my attempts to contrive an apology resulted in this spewing rampage. At this point in his own life, spewing was all that was left. I understood his reaction, but I could not bear it. I could not bear it anymore to be that scapegoat and carry transgressions on my head that were not mine to carry. I could not die in the desert.

That's when I turned the corner. That's when I called out for help. That's when I dialed 911 because nobody was there to help me. I was so broken and so confused and so hurt I didn't even remember dialing it until days after it happened.

911 works a lot better than some of my friends. They come to your house right away. They ask you what's been going on. They take notes and meet with each of you separately. They give advice and they give warnings.

They also put you on record.

Someone who knows my ex told me that as I dialed the number, I looked into my husband's eyes and said, "You're coming down." I don't remember saying that. I don't remember that I would even talk like that. But if I did, it was the gutsiest thing I had spoken in all three decades of our marriage.

The Take-Over

After the call to 911, the dynamics changed. Our charade fell apart. We could no longer hide anything from our daughter. I packed my bags and two days after the worst Christmas on the planet, I went on what I thought might become an extended visit to my brother's house four states away. Only a week into the visit and the Lord told me to go home and "take back my space." I had no idea what that meant but took the first plane home and discovered my husband was out of town and a woman from the church was house-sitting. I told her I was home now, thank you, and she left the house in my care. I put away the decorations left from Christmas, cleaned out the fermenting refrigerator contents, fed one very happy dog and changed the sheets on the bed. I found my space.

By the time he came back to town, my husband had learned of my take-over and only came back to get his own belongings—never alone and always with a cohort. I told him he could stay downstairs, just like before, but of course nothing was like it was before and he moved in with some friends. All direct communication ceased and anything he wanted from me was related to me through any one of three of his friends, the ones I referred to as "the talking heads."

While we were married, if there was something my husband did not like that I was doing, he would either leave me a letter or a cassette tape recording of what he did not like and why he did not like it. We did not talk; I was confronted with something two-dimensional to contend with. It wasn't until years after the divorce that I realized these methods of communication allowed him the ability to form his thoughts and disappointments in me into a well-formed and well-constructed paragraph or phrase. And he didn't have to look at me when he said it. And it left me no comeback.

In truth, seeing a letter or cassette with my name on it reminded me of that knuckled finger of my Dad's striking me in the back of the head. I had no mother who could wrap her arms around me and take away the pain, so I turned to the Lord for wisdom.

Why isn't He Plan A in everything we do, anyway?

Weathering The Storm

I stayed in the house while storms swirled around it: F5 tornadoes, category five hurricanes, bowling ball-size hail, immeasurable depths of snowfall. That's when the assaults were thrown and all the rumors started. I did my grocery shopping between four and five in the morning so I wouldn't run into anybody I knew. I spent most days crying in anguish while the storms raged, praying for a quick and painless death of one sort or another. My memory has allowed the days to fade as dimly as the light that came from my eyes during that season of storms.

Somehow I managed to keep myself and the house clean, the dog walked and fed and my prayer life and devotional time intact. I had only two things to say to the Lord about the situation: I will not divorce this man and I cannot move from this house. Then I went back into my perpetual state of disbelief and inordinate grief.

The loudest of the talking heads called me with only one thing to say: If I would allow my husband to divorce me, he would give me the house.

Sometimes answered prayer is bittersweet, but it's answered, none-the-less.

Divorce Is...

(based on my own experience and not infringing on what has happened to others)

- Legalized abandonment.
- Two dead bodies—no grave, no memorial service, all mourning
- What God says He hates.
- Making what God intends null and void.
- A denial of the power of God to transform and redeem.
- Telling God **how** instead of asking Him **what**.
- Showing your children, by example, that God has allowed you to leave your spouse and that not all of those laws necessarily apply to everybody.
- Blame, shame, and lame, in that order.
- Something breaking UP that has nothing UP about it.
- Something coming DOWN because that's the only direction left.
- A deliberate choice to leave a relationship that, if allowed, could nurture and sustain two human beings and bring them to the place of Christ-likeness they each claim to seek.
- The second original great divide, closely following the first one found in the third chapter of Genesis.

135

- The fastest way to lose every other meaningful relationship you've ever had.

- An unstable foundation poured out for the next generation to build on, like it or not.

- A spouse on their deathbed, looking into the eyes of the one they vowed to love for all eternity and with their very last breath and final ounce of energy, giving them the finger. (This is harsh and raw, but so is ripping apart something that is supposed to stay in one piece.)

- Splitting in two what is supposed to be one.

- Sometimes a necessary rescue plan.

Chapter Seven

almost caved

Take My Breath Away

You know that feeling you get when you just wake up and don't know where you are or what day it is? You know how it goes away in just a few seconds, when your mind awakens just enough to remind you of where you are and that you just came out of a dream?

I hate it when that happens.

I usually lay there and separate my dream from reality and when I've finally worked it through to where it all makes sense, I'm at peace. Sometimes I can even go back to sleep.

Something like that happened at the beginning of my recovery. I was living alone for the first time, just days into the new journey. I was asleep, or maybe not, and heard the sound of footsteps walking down the hallway towards the bedrooms. The outside doors were locked and yet I sensed it was my husband who had come into the house. I heard him as he opened my bedroom door and stood right next to me. He quietly leaned over and took the extra pillow by my head, put it on my face, and held it there. I opened my eyes and saw only the darkness of the pillow being pressed firmly into my face.

But I could breathe.

I wasn't at all sure if I was awake or asleep. It didn't really matter. What mattered was that I could breath.

I remember sitting straight up in bed and finding no pillow on my face, no one in the room, and no one in the house.

"Lord, what was that all about?"

"Honey, he's going to try to kill your spirit, but did you notice you could breathe?"

Spy Games

It's easy to get paranoid and think people are spying on you when they are, in fact, spying on you.

In ministry, we thought this was a good thing to do. Spy. But we didn't call it that because that doesn't sound nice. Here's how it worked: if you thought someone was involved in sin or was heading in the wrong direction, you would report their activities to the group leader or go directly to one of the pastors and turn in a "report"—which, now being so much clearer to me, was an *evil* report.

It all seemed to make sense, except for one little problem. The spy tactics rarely came out of relationship and nearly always seemed to be based entirely on judgment. The whole thing would have made a lot more sense if it had been life and death stuff, but most of it wasn't. I would never say we never cared for each other or held a concern. I believe we cared very much. What we did with that care and concern seemed to circumvent what should have been relational and made it a matter for the elders or the pastors to know and resolve.

But we didn't distinguish that difference between concern and judgment because that wasn't the way we were trained.

My high school driver's education instructor insisted we call his course Driver Education, not Driver Training. He would say *"You train dogs, you educate people."*

We were not educated properly. But we were well trained.

The church presented us with what we thought to be a wonderful way to help our teens through their tumultuous years. We paired each of them with a rock-solid twenty-something who would be their listening ears. That made sense, too, since the last ears a teen wants to speak to are located on each side of the head of both parents.

The only problem with that kind of thinking became evident when the twenty-something heard something they believed the pastor ought to know about. That's where the judgment thing came in again and tales were told that might have been better shared in the home. I do believe pastors may have wisdom for a situation, but when they sit in the family unit and take the place of a parent, I get uneasy.

The fruit of this kind of practice came when we discovered a young boy in the church was being sexually abused by one of our own Sunday school teachers. When the poor little boy finally got the nerve to tell his sister what was happening to him, she bypassed her parents and went straight to the pastor with the information.

That kind of thinking permeated the church and we never saw it as being abnormal.

We were just doing what we were trained to do.

Woof!

It was the summer before our teenage daughter was to leave for Bible school. She could tell our marriage dynamics had taken a deadly turn.

Trying to pretend things were fine wasn't working.

She found solace in having someone else's ears and turned to her twenty-something mentor on a daily basis. She spent the majority of the time conversing, I later learned, about how wonderful her daddy was and how demonic her mother was, as she had been told over and over by Daddy that Mom was.

Out of the blue, the Lord spoke to me and told me that everything my daughter was sharing was being reported back to the new pastor through her mentor.

I called this woman myself. My hands were shaking and my heart was pounding out of my chest. I love hearing from the Lord. It is my desire to obey Him. I'm not happy when I'm asked to step out of my comfort zone, but I knew I had to confront it. I asked her outright if everything my daughter was telling her was being reported back to the new senior pastor, who by now had replaced my husband. She confessed, angrily, that it was, and my timid response, based more in sadness than in anger, was to say, "That's information for a parent to know, not a pastor." That's about as bold as I was able to be at that time. I was still in the early stages of learning to say what needed to be said, and resting confidently in it.

After the bus crash, the church made an announcement to the congregation that included only what they wanted them to know about what was really happening in our household. Apparently the pastor also announced that anyone in a relationship with me should stay in that relationship. That's what I was told, anyway. In actuality, only two of my friends ever stayed connected or called or visited me, and when they did, it was always uneasy and terribly awkward due to a rather large, grey elephant sitting in the room. Ten years later, nothing has changed, and for the first time I am wondering if the pastor really said that.

Then there is that awful thought about what might just be the truth of the matter.

"They weren't really your friends," many people have told me over the years. I have always believed, and continue to believe, they really do love me, but they were just well trained.

It has been the history of the leadership that if you approached them with any kind of admonition or correction, you were considered as either deceived or a traitor, and traitors got the silent treatment. I myself had given the silent treatment to everyone who left my church with a complaint and, yes, I know, I was reaping what I myself had sown. And yes, I have indeed repented. And yes, maybe that silent treatment policy has been changed in my old church, but I can only relate what was happening to me at that time.

The crash left me severely damaged, with the worst injuries coming straight at my heart. They were a double-whammy known as rejection and isolation, a torture unlike anything I have ever known. Jesus went into the Garden of Gethsemane and no one went with Him because they were overtaken with sleep. Their priorities were off. Their flesh gave way. In a sense, too, my friends also slept. And while I of course did not personally sweat blood, I knew anguish of heart. I remember days spent lying on the floor, wailing loudly because loud was what I did and wailing was all I had left.

My husband had left me, my daughter had moved out and wasn't talking to me except through occasional e-mails detailing how evil and demonic I was. And now my brothers and sisters in Christ had abandoned me. The church took its toll inwardly as it divided itself into two camps—for or against the decisions that were made in the leadership. Later, it would divide again, as confused and disheartened members left to find a place to heal.

A double-whammy. As if the bus crash were not already a disaster, then it tumbled down a steep embankment, adding more injury and calamity.

There was no Camp-Carol, it seemed, until one exception showed up; this one bright light that flickered just a speck in my darkness; this one person from my home church showed me great kindness after the bus crash. She was someone I did not know well, but she seemed to come out of nowhere, and always with food. A local supermarket provided my church with donated foods that were distributed to the needy and my name was put on their list. I felt so much better, knowing I was at the very least being thought of.

The woman called me regularly. She visited often. She exhibited care and concern—two things now lacking in my life to the point of desperation. I shared all my thoughts and feelings with her, believing she would understand that I wasn't the bad guy here. Week after week, she came to my house, bearing the food and the fellowship I needed and craved. And she asked a lot of questions, to which I had a lot of answers.

Then one day, out of the blue, she called and said the food was no longer being distributed to the church (it was) and she would not be coming to my house again (she didn't). I later learned she had already turned in enough material to satisfy the requirements the pastors had asked of her.

Her assignment was done and I was alone again.

I call her the mole.

Hell Bent

Before her "duty" was finished, the mole came to my house one day all excited. She had just had a wonderful experience and wanted to share it with me. It concerned one of those "divine encounters," she said, and a real opportunity to share the Gospel. I urged her to tell me more.

I don't remember any of the details about why she was where she was. I don't remember her telling me anything that led to such an intense discussion about Jesus. I do know that my old church was hell-bent on getting everybody saved and it was the only topic being preached at the podium for months on end. Or so I was told.

Here's what I DO remember. I do remember that the two men she shared with were in a drug rehab program. I tried to imagine the joy that would have emanated from that discussion, how it would bring such a welcome relief, how totally life-changing it could be.

I also remember, and far too clearly, the joy she was experiencing right there in my kitchen as she related to me how successful the talk had become.

"Were you able to pray with them, to lead them to the Lord?" I asked.

"No, but I was able to do the next best thing."

"And what was that?"

"I left them knowing that if they died, they were going to hell."

Out Of Ammunition

My first Goliath-type battle began when a pastor called me into his office to give me a "heads up." My husband had written a letter to all the area pastors to warn them about me. This particular pastor was the only one who felt it necessary to tell me what was going on behind my back. I asked him to make me a copy of that letter and at one point in the healing process, some two or three years later, I threw that copy into a bonfire, where it belonged.

It contained a detailed account of my inability to face my sins and my intense rebellion against doing the will of God. It warned the pastors that listening to me defend my position or explain "my side of the story" was not only allowing them to partake in a lie straight from the pit of hell, but the demons who controlled me would fasten themselves onto the listener, should they, God-forbid, be in agreement with anything that came out of my mouth.

That same week, the elders and their wives from my church had an emergency meeting to warn them about my present behavior, making it very clear that "she is crazy; let us pray for the healing of her mind."

It was at this point I envisioned myself confronting said

pastors and elders and their wives, who at one time were my friends, and telling them the very good news that surely they already must know—that I was neither demonized nor insane.

The vision I had lacked substance. The vision lacked credibility. The vision lacked, period. Word was out, I was labeled and the journey through hell was well on its way.

I was in no position to confront my accusers. They already believed the reports, which didn't say much for me, and any attempt to assure them of its absurdity resulted in my looking more the fool than the foolish stories they were told.

"Hi, it's me – Carol. And guess what? I've got great news for you: I'm not crazy!"

The Lord had now made it impossible for me to defend myself. He does these kinds of things. And while the abuse and misuse of spiritual positioning continued, I, in my frustration, impatience, and immaturity, determined that my spiritual calling was to kill it.

Unlike David, I had not yet killed a lion or a bear, but was sure I was called to take on a giant called Religion.

I carried five smooth stones in my pocket and began to toss them, one at a time, at what I thought surely must be my enemy.

I ran out of ammunition that same week.

A Four-Letter Word

God had warned me about all that was happening to me in the nightmare I had earlier—shortly after the carpet stain dream—about my husband moving furniture to cover it. I woke from this appalling second dream, trembling—feeling completely violated. I had just been gang-raped by the men in our church eldership.

That 4-letter word—rape—has a punch to it that goes beyond what most of those other 4-letter words we gasp at manage to produce. So in telling you I had this dream and the elders of my church gang-raped me, I decided maybe I ought to be a bit more specific and a bit more cautious. There is too much power in that word. But that IS the most fitting word, and by definition, rape is almost always an abuse of power rather than just a sexual act. (In recalling the dream, I remember that two of the elders did not join in but did watch what was going on and did nothing. Telling...).

"Rape," the dictionary definition, is described as "a violent, destructive and abusive treatment of something" and "an act of seizing somebody and carrying him or her away by force." Wow! How can you describe something volatile and repulsive and demeaning happening against a child of God by a number of men in a power position and limit yourself to one physical picture? I can only think: gang-rape.

My dream came to me early on in my journey, when I knew the elders were making and passing judgments about me. I did not make up that dream, and I have always believed the Lord to be in the dream, to give me an idea of what was taking place *purely on a spiritual level,* and not on a natural one. My dream was of a real rape, and it was a violation of the deepest kind. It takes away your personhood and your femininity, and it leaves you wondering if it was your fault, and you are never the same again. And it takes a very long time to trust again...especially men, and especially men in a power position.

I do have respect for church leaders, absolutely, but when they walk in that kind of spiritual abuse, women, especially, feel something beyond violation. And it doesn't just go away when the act has ended. It can leave the victim crippled emotionally and/or diseased and/or carrying around an inward life that is intended to originate out of love, not a violent act.

In the same way we can destroy a person's character by accusing and passing false judgment, so this power position can do exactly the same thing.

Bus Crash Injuries

I had already been broken down in my childhood by my father, uncle, and priest, but the Lord had re-built me by His saving mercies. Now it was happening again.

Within a short period of time, I was divorced by my husband of 31 years, excommunicated by my church of 30 years, and abandoned by my only child. Friends snubbed me on the street. My finances and medical coverage were taken away, my reputation in the Christian community was shot, and even my dog and cat managed to die during this time period. I tell people I never lost my truck because I didn't own one. ☺

The experience of abandonment and aloneness nearly cost me my true sanity. But He knew there was no way I could live in the atmosphere of that church and survive with the truth that

had been revealed to me, so He took me out and led me into the wilderness.

There are so many people out there like me who have been broken up or broken down by legalism. I see in my mind's eye a puppet all broken up, with its body parts strewn and caught in the strings and I think about how much like a puppet I felt—that old Stepford Wife thing—that control brings. Even if you get loosed from the control, you are still not going to be complete until you find "Body parts" who will help affirm your faith and help make you whole again—no strings for performance attached!

It took a full two years before I believed I wasn't living in deception again.

Mother's Day Blues

Mother's Day came and went without a card. I did get a call, however, explaining the absence.

"I'm spending the day with Daddy."

Now I know it's good not to hide and harbor ill will so I let her know it hurt me to be ignored. She laid down the "pure and simple" facts for me: I am totally responsible for the divorce as well as all her adult issues and mistrust of human beings and that she will never get counsel because she is right and I am deceived. I deserve this kind of treatment. "Oh yes and Daddy feels sorry for you and hopes you have a spiritual epiphany showing you how wrong you've been and how evil you are."

The next day, still suffering from the hangover I got from drinking in all that sour wine, I opened up to my daily devotion entitled *Made Perfect Through Suffering* and was reminded that Jesus didn't want the cup but drank it anyway.

Gulp.

Sunday

It used to be my favorite day. Today is Saturday and I dread tomorrow. I just want Monday to come and then I won't have to think about why I hate Sundays for several more days.

As the pastor's wife, I would greet the flock, love on the kids, and stand proud next to my man with the high calling. I was born for the job. Actually, I was born-again for the job. It fit me, or so I thought, to a T.

I never imagined that a divine encounter with God would leave me divorced, shamed, and alone. I never thought I would have nowhere to go that was safe and accepting and uplifting. I never thought I would hate Sundays.

Lord, I still love *You*. It's just Your day that I dread.

Still, the others are not so great, either.

I miss it, I miss them, I miss it all. I loved that place and those people for nearly all my Christian life. Can't go back, can't move forward.

My plan is to hide in You until Sunday is like every day and every day is good.

A part of me understands that to be true, but right now my broken heart is having a hard time coming into alignment with that.

I Was There

I was there when they pulled the plug on your dad and we watched the monitor together and saw the numbers go down until the line went flat. And we wept because he died and maybe because we didn't see the miracle we'd hoped for.

I was there when the doctor told you to have a D&C because your baby was dead and I took you to my gynecologist for another opinion and she told us your baby was not dead and now she is a beautiful woman with a booming career and a miraculous start.

I was there when they took your husband to the emergency room and told us he needed brain surgery immediately and I took care of your three children until you could. He survived and you had three more children in celebration of life.

I was there when your first-born son was pronounced dead at the scene of the accident. He was the same age as my daughter, and we all knew 16 was just too young to die. We stayed up all night and talked about his short-lived, bittersweet life.

I was there when the cancer took your son just days shy of his 19th birthday and a whole community wept. The TV reporters asked me how you were doing because he was a star athlete, and I told them Jesus was holding all of us together because I didn't know what else to say.

I was there with you for those dozen years we prayed for a miracle baby. The doctor's told you it could only happen with their help, but you never needed their help, after all, to become the parents of two beautiful daughters.

I was there when you had your chemo or your radiation, not because I had to but because I wanted to. You needed me there and that was enough for me.

I was there to give you a baby shower for your first pregnancy and made it the best one ever even though it was killing me that you got pregnant on your first try, and I was still childless after eight years. I learned more than you'll know from obeying Him.

I was there when you turned 50. I got in touch with all your friends and told them you needed a new piano, and everybody cared enough to pitch in and tell you we loved you enough to make that happen.

I was there when you thought he might be the "right one" and we prayed together that you would know. You knew and he was.

In the early years when we were all so young, I was there when you got married, right beside you as your Matron of Honor or one of your bridesmaids, all fourteen of you lovely brides, and I watched you take your vows. I held your bouquet of flowers with my own the same way I held your heart to mine as we prayed together that first time. All fourteen of you, my friends.

I was there when you held that little boy in your arms and called him your son because we were able to make the right phone calls and know the right people to make you parents for the first time.

I was there when you received a prophetic word that I knew was the answer to your heart's desire and now, it was my desire, too.

I was there when you came to my house with a dish-to-pass and we watched the Bills lose the Super Bowl again or the ball drop on another year or our country have another birthday or any other reason we could think of to get together and eat.

I was there at the front of the church every New Year's Eve, reading the world's longest poem about everything that happened that year in our church family and getting it all to rhyme and you all told me, every year, this poem was my best one yet.

I was there worshipping with you every Sunday morning, with my hands in the air and my heart filled with such joy to be called to help shepherd the flock, standing beside the man I believed would always stand beside me.

At the exact time I am writing this tribute, a 26-year-old Army Sergeant, a young man from my old church, is being laid to rest. He was killed serving his country in the war in Afghanistan. Because his parents no longer speak to me, I have chosen to stay home this morning. They are very private people and I don't wish to embarrass them. Thirty-nine years ago, I led the young man's father to the Lord.

So even though I am sitting at my computer, in my heart, I am there at the funeral and my ears hear the bagpipes playing "Amazing Grace."

I always knew how to laugh with you when the joys and the blessings of the Lord were so rich we pinched ourselves to see if we were alive or if this was actually heaven.

I always cried with all of you and held you tight and wished to God I knew how to say and do the right thing because your pain was so extreme and I'd never done this kind of thing before and wanted to get it right.

It was never my job. It was always my life.

Hello Again

The light on my phone machine was blinking on and off again. Private Caller had left practically the same message. I was about to be slammed—again.

She told me she was delighted to know that I was all alone. She told me again that everything wrong I ever did or said in my life was coming back to me and offering me the miserable life I deserved. She expressed her joy that I would never see my granddaughter grow up which she said is good because I would have done a better job raising my daughter if I had gone to a casino on Sundays instead of attending church. She reminded me again that since my daughter was adopted, she wasn't really mine so there could be no "real love" between us, anyway. She concluded again that I was the rottenest person in the whole wide world.

I was still at the place emotionally where I thought she wasn't much off the truth.

Ring-Ring

Unknown Caller was on a roll. I was home for this one.

It was the day after another pajama day, which, lately, was coming twice a week instead of once. These are the days when life isn't worth putting clothes on for.

That morning before the call, I decided to put on clothes and go to the ladies meeting that meets on a Tuesday morning. I never know what to call it because it's sometimes a prayer meeting and sometimes a Bible study and mostly, I have concluded, simply more like a real church meeting experience than an actual, as-we-know-it church meeting. At this particular gathering, somewhere between the worship and the sharing, I went through major meltdown number 784, but who's keeping track?

I had to pray again—pray to turn my life over to Christ, again—pray for forgiveness for not believing God, again—pray He would give me what it was I was asking for, again, and believe, again, that He loved me enough to answer me in the affirmative, or anything close to it.

By the end of the meeting, I had allowed the Lord to put the symbolic wedding ring back on my finger.

Unknown Caller picked that same day to call again, within minutes after arriving home from the meeting. I picked up the phone and heard the one-word message of a sick-hearted woman.

"Unloved."

And then Unknown Caller hung up.

I hate how the devil uses the broken to break people even more.

Screwed

I suppose the best part of being admitted to a mental facility was that the not-so-friendly policeman felt I was okay enough not to be handcuffed. I appreciated that.

It was embarrassing enough to have a neighbor call the police because I was deeply depressed and she had tried to kill herself at least twice when she was deeply depressed and so of course I was going to take my life, too. It was useless trying to convince a policeman that just because you're crying and confused doesn't mean you're suicidal; it made me look goofier than the situation itself.

I soon learned that once you put the label on the jar, you get screwed at the top.

It proved to be a rather unpleasant visit, actually. I have yet to confirm it, but I was first placed, I am almost certain, in the original room used to film the movie, Snake Pit. While waiting for a bed to open up, I saw piles of patients begin to fill the hallway to overflowing. Apparently there were no available beds and this was the waiting area. They set up my bed next to a man who spent the majority of his time enjoying his own sexuality.

I was embarking on a journey that began with a judgment on my head and a new set of rules.

I remember, too, that the moon was full. Of course it was.

The label was on the jar.

The daily headaches, caused from a lack of caffeine that only coffee would cure, were the only physical pain I experienced. At one point, when they finally found a room for me, it was void of anything with points or pills and had bars on the windows.

At least I was alone.

I sensed grace, beyond anything I knew.

It was a Catholic hospital and when I asked for a Bible, no one could find one for me to read. Half the patients there claimed to be a Christian. I found both things unnerving.

Early on in my visit, I asked a nurse where I would be eating my meals. She pointed to a room full of mentally ill people in a comatose state and told me I would eat in there. "With them?" I asked, to which she replied with a grin that bore a strong resemblance to Nurse Ratchet in *One Flew over the Cuckoo's Nest*,

"Honey, you're one of them."

Screwing that lid just a little tighter.

By the time the doctors came to see me, four days had gone by and I was feeling a lot like a criminal. Apparently, doctors don't work weekends, and my admittance day was poorly timed. A Monday morning examination concluded that a mistake had been made putting me there and I would be free to go home after the customary 48-hour wait that followed the examination.

They advised I work through my grieving process, and any crying out to the Lord needed to be done with my inside voice. A counseling session or two couldn't hurt, either.

I had been stuck there for a full week.

By then, the word was already out that Carol's been locked up.

Once you put the label on the jar, everyone reads it.

HARD TO REJOICE

Jesus, I know
   Scripture says
We are supposed to praise You always.
   Rejoice always
Is the command,
   In everything give thanks.
That means everything, we are told.

Those whom You've used
   To bring hope to the world,
   The Corries and Jonis,
Are people who live by that principle
   So it is true.
And I know I should, too.

But I feel
   more like a Jeremiah.
I see only the things that
   Cause me to lament.
Yes, there are great miracles
   Happening.
Lives are turning to You
   Every day.
People sing with joy and are
   Lifted into worship to You.
I enter the Holies with them, too.

But it's hard for me
   To always rejoice
When the pure is
   Mixed with impurities;
When the place of refuge
   Inflicts its own wounds;
When supposed unity
   Is divided by discord,
   Or is forced under tyranny;
When the voice of Your wisdom
   Is heathen tinged;
When leaders look the wrong way
   And lead many astray;
When we have to wait a lifetime
   To know the fruit.

Can you rejoice, Jesus?
   Do You smile?
Or do You mourn
   As I do?

Jesus,
When You
look out over Your sheep
Do you ever weep?

     Cheryl Zehr July 1997
  (After an almost fatal church wounding)

An Admission Of Guilt

If the recipe I am following says, *add 1/2 cup flour*, I measure a half a cup of flour and not one third or two thirds of a cup. Same for teaspoon measurements. I follow the rules—somebody knows better than I do about this recipe. I don't do improvisation, second guessing, or smidges. Never had and probably never will. Same goes with medicine. If the directions on a medicine bottle says, *take 2 tablets every 4 hours*, I take two tablets every four hours and if need be, another two, but only after exactly four hours has passed. Somebody knows better about what is harmful, or not, to my body.

This is my introduction to my three attempts at taking my life.

I could easily have downed a bottle of something, sliced a vein-y area with one of my guaranteed-for-life knives, or put a bullet into my gun. Yes, I have a gun. But I never even thought of these methods because it wasn't in the plan or "recipe."

Instead, three times I sat in my car with the engine running and the garage door closed. All three times I was sad and all three times I was crying hysterically. All three times, the engine ran for less than two minutes, while I set my head to realizing this was equivalent to gauging a measurement, or to taking 4 tablets every 2 hours—double the dose in half the time. It might be harmful. All three times, I knew I wouldn't do it. All three times, I cried out to You and asked You to take away the sadness and the pain.

None of them would I call a "suicide attempt." I would call them a child pouting because I was two years old and wasn't getting my way. I would call them being a teenager and slamming the door and saying, "I hate you," on the way out. I would call them stomping my foot, kicking the door, and saying really bad words all at the same time.

All of them were cries for help that could only be heard by one listening ear.

Daddy, Abba, Father, Papa.

He would call it Healing.

I call Him *Healer.*

Section Four

Break Through

"...I have broken the bands of your yoke and made you walk upright." Leviticus 26:13b

Chapter Eight

In Desperate Need

Failure To Thrive

I watch the woman stroke her fingertips along the area and I am acutely aware of how gentle her touch is. Her fingers sway softly from side to side, and then up and down and she is concentrating intently on the area where her fingers are moving. Her eyes anticipate a response.

I know she is just holding an iPod, but I find myself wondering if someone would please touch me as gently as she is touching this small instrument that has become our world's latest form of communication.

To touch, I want to believe, is communication, but if I tell you I want someone to touch me, you might not understand. It's been perverted so much, I fear we've forgotten what kind of touch I'm talking about and just how pure and necessary it really is. Our schools forbid it, but children still need it. Babies fail to thrive without it and sometimes they die from lack of it.

I, too, have been slowly dying since the bus crash.

Hug me, stroke my arm, shake my hand, pat my back, give me a high-five. I want to feel skin again. All I crave is what I no longer get.

Please someone, just touch me.

When no one does, I save up a little cash and allow myself a professional body massage. I weep through the entire thirty minutes.

"That's okay, "the woman tells me. "It happens a lot."

Touch

"Breathe in and say, '*I am...*' Breathe out and say '*...healing.*'"

These were the instructions my massage therapist gave me. I follow instructions well.

She had me in her hands for a full hour, the result of a fitting birthday gift from a friend, a friend familiar with the aches and pains I sustained in that infamous bus crash. Words that cut had found their landing strip in the deep places and marked their damage in muscle cramps and tightened joints and frayed nervous systems.

So I lay, fully exposed, on her very expensive cot and the therapist positions her palms and fingertips to assist me in this very hands-on healing process. I do as she says.

I breathe in and think, "*I am.*"

I breathe out and think, "*...healing.*"

I do this for about ten minutes. I am not sure her fingers will find where my soul is but I am content and I am relaxing and I am thinking the right thoughts, until the Lord interrupts them with what I can only describe as a kind of voice-over.

And I hear him say, "*I am,*" as I breath in; I hear Him say, "*Healing,*" as I breathe out. He has the louder voice now, and I hear Him say the words over and over as I continue to breathe in and to breathe out, and He touches me in a place her fingers never find.

You Turns

There are a lot of people in this world who do a lot of wonderful things in their life and all we remember is that they killed someone and hid the body in the backyard.

So what if they paid their bills, fathered three delightful children, and never cheated on their wife or their income tax? It's not the good we recall but the one horrific act that determines how we remember them.

It seems to cancel out all the good rather swiftly.

I'm always stunned when they interview a mother whose son was just arrested for murdering his best friend in a bar. "He's really a good boy," she says, and I quietly question her definition of good. Someone I know personally had a son who stole from his grandmother, impregnated three girls, grew marijuana in his back yard, and sold drugs on the street. She told me he was really a good boy.

I told her, "No, he's not a good boy, but he does have a nice personality." Mr. Personality served 10 years in prison.

My ex-husband was certainly no murderer. He preached for three decades with an anointing that touched and helped unknown numbers of people. He paid his tithes, took care of his family and the flock for a quarter of a century, and was, without question, a hard and dedicated worker. And while he did a lot of wonderful things with me and for me and to me, I also remember what he did to destroy that and how it all came to one horrific end.

It seems, it canceled out the good rather swiftly.

Much of the evil talk and treatment I endured the last few years of my marriage, I firmly believe, are a result of my ex-husband's inability to admit his own insecurities and mistakes and allow the Lord to heal the reason why he was unable to admit they existed in the first place. It gave the enemy a long air strip on which to land his plane.

My intentions in saying this should not be interpreted as male or husband bashing. I believe wounded people respond in different ways to their own wounding in order to conceal their own hurt. One of these responses to injury very often appears as arrogance; another might manifest as a domineering, controlling attitude. Others turn inward and become mute and docile. These are more like reactions than responses and they are common to man. However, none of these responses promote what we really need: healing.

My ex had to defend himself and his situation and if he were not the one at fault, as he claimed rather boisterously, then it had to be everyone else who was wrong and it was his job to "fix" us.

And it remains, sadly, the way I remember him even now. He hurt a lot of people, me included. I feel truly sorry for him. He now has two broken marriages behind him and while the first might not have been saved, I still believe the second one had the potential for restoration. The stings I received from his final outbursts were signs of his own brokenness.

What he doesn't realize is that there are hundreds of people he has left behind who still love and miss him. I would be remiss if I didn't say I was one of them.

What the Lord is teaching me is that no evil deed ever really cancels out what we call the good deeds. We don't have black and white boxes balancing on the scale of justice. The sacrifice on the Cross covers it all; we just need to see our need and embrace Him. Our struggle seems to be with seeing we have a need in the first place and understanding the grace that comes with admitting it.

That, I believe, is the point where self ends and transformation begins.

By Definition

The Definition Of **Bittersweet** Is:

Falling in love and knowing it is forever

Having a family you know loves you and will be there for you no matter what

Being Mom to a precious girl you simply adore

Enjoying the fellowship and intimacy of a wonderful group of Christian brothers and sisters

Living in a town that fits who you are and knows who you are and accepts who you are

Being able to pay the bills every month

Losing all of the above

Remembering all of the above

Hearing the sound of your own heart breaking

Living with that loss

Knowing it is lost forever

Realizing it is better that way.

That is, clearly, the definition of *bittersweet*.

Make Me Like You

Right after the bus crash, and long before I started getting the victory, I shut off all the sounds around me that reminded me of church. Every worship song came with a vision and the vision only reminded me of my losses. I resorted to finding a new song—to listen only to music I never heard before, so there would be no association, no connection that could sweep me back into a place of inordinate sadness. One of the songs I play most often had a repeated line that said, "Make me like you," and of course, it is the desire of every Christian to be made into His image and likeness: Make me like YOU.

But that's not what my ears heard.

I heard, "Make me LIKE you," because, as frightening as the thought was, I didn't much like the Lord; He wasn't always giving me warm fuzzies.

There was much about Him that my flesh was not particularly fond of and it took some time for me to discover it was okay to feel that way. He's not going to up and leave me because of this. The important thing was that I recognized it's part of that relationship thingy.

Still, He was nothing like I thought He would be. He rarely

lived up to my expectations and too often I think He hid from me and kept far too many secrets and didn't always make clear pathways for me to walk on. He pushed me WAY past that point of "more than I can bear" and then He pushed me again.

He appeared to let the devil come in and do the Job thing.

Every day in the shower, I found myself checking out my overweight and age spot-saturated torso for boils. Of course, they never came.

My mother used to hang a poster in her apartment that thoroughly annoyed me. It showed a ragdoll caught in the middle of the wringer on one of those old style washing machines our grandmothers used mid-century. Underneath the picture, it read: *The truth will set you free, but first it will make you miserable.*

I hated that poster and thought it bordered on sacrilege. Then I walked with the Lord a few decades and learned, well, truth. And the truth is, we must all learn how to be honest and open with the Lord, and in being honest, we will know real pain. Which, frankly, I still find to be a real pain, but then I am still growing and that is a good sign that there is still life in the old girl.

Pain, in the end, is productive, like childbearing. Fighting it is counterproductive. Screaming out loud sounds better when you turn it into a book chapter.

Read on. I still have a lot of screaming to do.

Stolen Sheep

A few weeks into the bus crash recovery, I started trying to attend church again. However, due to that horrible letter, I was not usually welcomed with warm greetings at a lot of the area congregations. I finally found a small quiet church that greeted me as if I were just a normal person so I began attending services there. I spent most of the time comparing their services to the ones I was used to and the rest of the time I just cried a lot. There were a few families in that church that used to attend mine. All of them left for the same reason—leadership control—and all of them were in various stages of healing.

But they were healing.

I got up the nerve to meet with the pastor and just laid out matter-of-factly to him all I had experienced with the Lord and how it got me to this place. I'm sure I also cried, as I could not tell the story without crying. Actually, nothing much has changed in the telling, even to this day, except the intensity of the cry. Lately, it is often just a whimper. And while the professionals were calling it PTSD, I only knew it to be excruciating grief.

I remember that he listened politely to me and said I would be welcomed at his church. I went home a little more at peace. I sucked in any form of kindness anyone expressed to me and he was kind.

That's when it happened. That's when I went into panic-mode and lost a good night's sleep. The pastor of that church was going to call up my pastors and report to them what I had just told him in that meeting. I knew that because that's what

172

pastors do. They tell on the flock. It shows you are out of order when you bare your soul like that to another pastor, and you must be reported and confronted and punished. It's an unwritten rule among pastors and shows your concern and your caring; you have no right stealing or counseling other pastors' sheep.

I tried with all my might to be brave and met the pastor head-on and asked him if he had told them about our conversation and he looked at me with such bewilderment and said, "Why would I?" I explained what we believed, based on all I knew, and the dear man just looked at me in a gentle way and simply said, "These are men who love God and I respect that. But as for reporting you to them, well, we just have different ways of dealing with situations and I can't understand or explain to you why they do that. It's nothing I would do or think to do."

I stayed and worshipped there for a few more weeks. The church carries good memories for me, even now, and while it was not home, it did allow the early stages of healing to happen.

Meat And Milk

The first time I realized I had to be gracious instead of right, I threw a hissy-fit.

I wrote in my journal. "How do I move past it and pretend I'm just fine? I'M NOT FINE! What did YOU do? You either turned your cheek, knocked a table over or went to the *Cross. I'd like to slap a cheek, turn over a table, and then go to the Cross and ask you for forgiveness.*"

I was new at living alone, new at hearing the Lord for myself and new at the business of deflecting nasty rumors being told about me, and handling complete and utter rejection by everyone I loved.

So I began searching the Word for vindication Scriptures.

The vindication Scriptures are a great reference point when you decide to be your own avenger. They stir up your juices and put arrows on your anger. They direct the arrows into the heart of the enemy and, if you aim just right, they can destroy your enemy.

I grabbed my Bible and sat on my backyard deck, the Bible in one hand and my morning coffee in the other. I read Psalm 35 out loud, raising my voice and putting emphasis on the parts I wanted the Lord to be especially attuned to.

"Stir up Yourself, and awake to my vindication."

"They opened their mouth wide against me and said, 'Aha, aha'…this you have seen, O Lord; so *do not keep silence.*"

"Vindicate me…according to your righteousness…let them be ashamed and brought to mutual confusion…let them be clothed with shame and dishonor."

I went back into the kitchen to refill my coffee mug and brought it out to the deck. The wind had turned the page of my opened Bible and my eyes instantly fell where it had opened, on Psalm 37:10.

"For yet a little while and the wicked shall be no more."

I was sure He was seeing things my way and searched for the "bring fire out of heaven" stuff. I was a mature Christian woman, feeding, I was confident, on the meat of the Word and learning to apply the written Word where it would do the most good, or, in actuality, do what I wanted it to do.

The Lord had reminded me of one thing—my enemies were indeed wicked.

Didn't the Lord just tell me that?

Whose wind blew that page, anyway?

The Lord quickly pulled this verse out of my memory bank, "Vengeance is Mine, I will repay," says the Lord (Romans 12:19).

The arrows of my words were never arrows at all, but boomerangs. Within a matter of just an hour or two, my words were coming straight back and hitting me dead center in the heart. The impact forced me to my knees as I was reminded it was the Lord who does the vindicating, that I was making the very judgments I sought to condemn others for making, which might make ME the one with the wicked thinking.

I crawled back to my journal and sheepishly wrote,

"Does this mean hang in there, MYOB*, *and stop playing judge?*"

"What do YOU think?" He asked.

I repented, wiping away tiny droplets of milk from the corners of my mouth.

* <u>M</u>ind <u>Y</u>our <u>O</u>wn <u>B</u>usiness

Cooking With Graham

A very dear friend, the same one who also gave me the massage gift certificate, introduced me to the sermons from a Godly prophetic man named Graham Cooke. She gave me a handful of cassette tapes and CD's just about the same time my mind and my emotions were about to take me to lalaland. It was also a time when the media was populated with announcers whose voices were accented with a British or Australian twang. Apparently they are an easy listen and he was an easy listen, this man from Great Britain who had recently settled in California. Easier still was the simple message he carried and one my spirit was longing to hear.

I started out with an insatiable appetite for the truth and these few cassette tapes. I would listen to him preach for, quite literally, hours on end, soaking in revelation and basking in the discovery of a God who didn't carry a sledge hammer in His right hand. I was also crazy about Graham's honesty and obscene sense of humor. He kept breaking religious rules and I loved that about him. For a few uneasy months, right after my divorce kicked in, I had a mad crush on the man.

There. I said it.

He married, I moved on and I never once settled into lalaland.

But it was fun to have a crush again.

British Invasion

When you want to give credit where credit is due, you thank God first and foremost and then mentally list all the "Body parts" who contributed to your success or healing or whatever it is you're giving credit for. Graham Cooke, I must really hand you the biggest thank you note of all. The sound of your voice carrying a revelation of grace was the real voice of truth for me.

The Lord brought him to America from England and he might be England's greatest contribution to the States. He had a message that burned on his heart and had its basis in this simple fact: God is incredibly kind and He loves you because He loves you because He loves you and He doesn't know how to do anything else but love you.

Google his name and learn more.

Somehow he managed to get that message on those tapes and CD's (which were often given to me as gifts) with multiple stories to back it up and with lots of British-style humor. I don't even remember the jokes. The message, however, is tattooed on my soul.

I spent my saddest four years playing about three dozen of Graham's CD's over and over again. Each time I would repeat a CD, it was as if I had never heard it before. It wasn't the length or the breadth that carried me away—it was the depth. The entanglements of my life began to unravel, the disillusionments became illuminated by grace, and the lies were replaced by truth. While it is not an overnight process, there is no doubt what he

said carried my heart into a place where I only knew grace and I only saw Jesus.

I began to like what I saw. I began to like Who I saw. I even began to like myself again.

While Graham might have been sent here for a variety of reasons, one of them surely was me.

An English Lesson, Part 1

Every moment spent in my car was another opportunity to listen to a Graham Cooke message. My friend had introduced me to him when my husband and I were still living together in the same house and pretending to the world that all was well with ours. Nobody knew we were living on two different levels of that Gingerbread house.

I used every opportunity I could to get away; it's not like running *from*, but hiding *in*. Listening to Graham's preaching was my hiding place, like a balm for my ears. The messages on those tapes caused a Great Exchange: truths I longed to hear were replacing lies I'd been led to believe.

Truth, however it comes, is welcoming and heart-warming and there was a time when truth felt so wonderful and so good and so liberating that I actually felt guilty about soaking in it. A liberated spirit is a soaring spirit.

So I listened to a lot of Graham and let my spirit soar. It literally took years for many of these truths to manifest; it had taken years for the lies to take root. I had made my soil fertile for all the wrong seeds.

An English Lesson, Part 2

I was doing the Graham Cooke exchange, caught up in a message about how the Lord was there to fill up those places within us that needed what we lacked. I was driving on a main highway and Graham was preaching to an auditorium-filled crowd. He asked each of them to close their eyes and I was so caught up in the message that I pulled over and parked in the first available parking lot. Graham has a way of making you listen and realize that maybe, just maybe, God has something to say to you that might be life-changing.

Graham asked his audience to consider whatever it was they had need of and believe God to supply that need with Himself. My lack-list was long and He could be just about anything to me at that point and a need would be met.

"I want you to close your eyes and ask the Lord what it is He intends to be for you and to you," we were instructed, *"And then I want you to allow Him to empty your mind and listen for the answer."*

Have you ever sat perfectly still and tried to clear your mind out of the thinking process and into a place of what I suppose they call true meditation?

"Okay, so now I'm not driving so I don't have to concentrate on the road.

"Good. Now I'm in the parking lot, the car is turned off and there's no one around looking at me and making me uncomfortable.

"Okay, so let me see what it is I need? I need affection, I need acceptance, I need money, I need... Wait. I need too much. If I go

over this list, I'll just be flooding my mind with more thoughts and it won't stop thinking and..."

It was at this point in time that I was, for just a split second, void of thought. He was about to tell me which need He was going to meet and I began to consider that my real need was to shut up.

His voice broke through my trivial clamor and I heard Him say one word, *just one word,* which left me totally devastated. It was a word I feared to hear, for it is not what I wanted Him to be for me.

"Husband," He said, as plain and as sure as any word I have ever heard.

I had known that word as a noun and now He was telling me it was time to examine it as a verb.

Sharing Sharon

The only way to have a relationship with Sharon is to share her.

I have to share her with her husband of nearly 50 years. I have to share her with her four children and their children and the nursery school she works at and the church she helps her husband pastor. And when we get time together on the telephone, which is the only place we get together, we are small children hiding out in a field, under a large tree with huge branches ever-so-gently leaning over to protect and conceal us from the rest of the world. It is here we share our stories and our pain; our secrets and our hearts. I am finally getting the big sister I have always wanted. She is finally getting the friend pastors' wives are rarely allowed time or opportunity to find.

I can say all these things about Sharon because I have learned to be confident in her love for me. I can read this story to Sharon and know she will be humbled and ever so grateful. She will also laugh and tell me she thinks I'm a "hoot."

Sharon was introduced to me by her brother. He knew I was looking for a friend and confidant and felt his older sister fit the criteria. The first time I walked into her house, the Lord told her where I walked was holy ground. Never have I thought of myself as *holy*, unless you want to change the spelling to *holey*. Then I might agree with you. She saw Christ in me. I was glad to hear He was still there and somebody could see Him.

Sharon, unlike me, is tall and thin. She carries herself with grace and dignity. The fluffy, short, white hair on her head is more like a crown than anything else. As my father used to say, "She has more class by accident than I have on purpose." But her classiness is no accident.

Whenever I call her, I always ask her if she is "with child," because nearly every time we talk she is either watching someone's children or with her own grandchildren. Miraculously, they seem to behave fairly well and long enough to allow us to indulge in a little conversation.

Since we first met, Sharon has become the pillow I grab for comfort, the Vaseline on all my boo-boos.

She always answers the phone with high energy no matter where she is or what she's doing, knowing it's me at the other end. We can be calmly discussing the events of the day and just as suddenly endorse it as an opportunity to intercede and then groan in the spirit for an hour. We can work a situation to death with our wit and our wisdom and reach a conclusion an hour later that nothing we said is worth diddly-squat. We miss each others' birthdays and don't care. It's about being super glued to each other, for better or for worse. It's not marriage but it's just as holy and just as committed and just as ordained of God.

My favorite memories of Sharon have been when I call her in the middle of the night in deepest despair. "I want you to call me if you need to pray. Even if it's in the middle of the night; I'm there for you," she promised. So I test her dedication.

She is always quick to the phone and quick to respond with what she believes to be divine advice. It's not until the next day, as we commiserated over the night before, she confessed she couldn't remember I had even called. I confess that everything she said made absolutely no sense, anyway.

But her promise was to be there and she didn't say to what depth or to what extent.

I think because I share her with so many others, I don't always get the best parts. Still, I love getting her leftovers and find they are more than adequate. I also think that what we have is friendship at its finest.

Sharon, I have concluded, is Jesus in a dress.

Chapter Nine

Missing Marriage

Man-Ic

The most romantic gesture I know was put to music when Barbra Streisand sang it on the first record album I ever paid real money for back in the 1960's. It seduced me with the notion that I could "...be the kind of girl designed to be kissed upon the eyes."

Those notions of romanticism went down the laundry shoot when my husband divorced me.

That first Valentine's Day that I had no valentine was a painfully lonely blur. In the year that followed, my days were spent watching the world around me through bowed, distorted glass, traveling circles in a goldfish bowl, and drowning in two cups of water. I busied myself with twelve months of distraction and made it to the following February 14th with the artificially induced idea to stage a NO-MAN-TIC dinner for all the widows and divorcees I knew.

I made a turkey dinner with all the trimmings and pretended I was over it. I was fine-thanks-for-asking. I encouraged my guests to write down their greatest struggle with their past loss and then lit a fire in my barbeque pit, burning the papers in a symbolic gesture that was really an attempt to appease a still-mourning hostess still hoping for reconciliation. It did nothing to change me personally, although my neighbor—the town judge—called to find out what the fire was all about and reminded me it was against the law.

Unbeknownst only to me, I was still in stage one of the mourning process.

I never reconnected with any of these women again on a personal basis.

I've been meaning to apologize to all of them.

By the time the third Lover's Day arrived, I had grimaced my way through the flowers and candy hoopla and made scrunched-up faces at all the commercials on my television set. That was the day I came home to find two dozen long-stemmed red roses between the front doors, with a little note saying I was loved. No one I knew took credit for the kindness but I saved the note and spent each successive Valentine's Day reminding myself that Jesus was the only man who would never leave me or forsake me.

I hope no one ever tells me who delivered the roses. I would like to think that angels make house calls.

Every successive February 14th, I close my eyes and He kisses them.

Time Out

It was my first date after the divorce. I had been alone several years and was both flattered and a nervous wreck. He was handsome, retired, and played guitar in a band. He was nothing like my ex.

Inside, I was screaming in my head, "Don't kiss me. Don't kiss me. Don't kiss me." Outside I was a babbling idiot.

Just minutes into the date, we were waiting for a table at a lakeside restaurant and I was still being my old self. My old self did not know how to be anything else. At that point, I had not realized the man had walked away from anything resembling Christianity for several years. The last time we had connected was in the Kingdom, decades before. We had reconnected at a mutual friends' retirement party. I was to learn his mental and spiritual state in a hurry.

He took off his $12,000 Rolex watch—he made sure to point that out, along with all the boats and cars he owned—and laid it on the bar we were leaning against and pointed to the big hand on the seven.

"See that big hand on the seven?" he asked.

I said yes I did.

"See where the nine is?" he asked again.

I said yes I did.

"*See if you can say anything at all that does not have God, church, or Christian in it by the time that big hand gets to the nine.*"

It was nice dating again for the millisecond it lasted.

Months later after another date I dared to venture on with another guy, I wrote in my diary, "I think he has a few loose screws. I don't feel called to tighten them."

On-Line Lures

I just wasted three easy monthly payments of $19.98 on a dating service that only added to my rejection by having perfect strangers tell me that "The distance is too great," which is another way of saying you're not worth the trip, honey.

Every morning was comparable to a cattle call as I opened up to new matches and checked them out head to toe to spirit. The fact that they might be doing the same thing with my profile never occurred to me until after the expiration date, but it had worked for a lot of my friends and it was possible it might work for me.

I ignored the men who were outright heathens or shorter than I. I already had a weight problem myself and wanted someone tall enough to make me look average-sized. I ignored the men who used the word *lonely* in their bio, or the ones who interspersed subtle or disturbing suggestions. These were the kinds of things that brought me to my knees as I begged the Lord to remove them from my very fragile mind. I considered myself to be wise and prudent, but I still asked for the gift of discernment.

I toyed with the idea that there existed, somewhere in the stratosphere, a retired millionaire looking for an insecure divorced woman who collected social security and carried more baggage than a movie starlet on vacation. He would, of course, also have a great sense of humor, perfect grandchildren, and no mortgage. He'd have all his hair and it would be soft and white and wavy. His teeth would be slightly protruded. He would be looking for company, companionship, and more cats. He had to like cats; there is no way I would part with them for something meaningful like a relationship.

I saw myself as a pretty good catch, not realizing that I was still in stage two of the grieving process and couldn't talk in a straight line. I maintained my sense of humor, a humor that landed me the grand title of Class Clown, 1964, Central

High. I was and always have been disease free, which nowadays is something people are looking for but still has no place in my own thinking process.

I could use a couple of crowns on my back molars, but at least I have my back molars. I have some age spots that are fun to watch grow and spread and some days I use them like a Rorschach test and try to figure out what their shapes look like. Except for the big toe on my right foot, my nails are long and pretty and are actually my own. That particular big toe, yes, the one I had surgery on to replace a joint, is another thing altogether, which shouldn't be located on a human being, actually, and unless it spreads, I probably won't do anything about it and will continue to camouflage it with a brightly colored nail polish.

I have a mortgage that will be paid up when I am in my mid-90s, which is about the same time I can stop working and retire. Other than that, my finances are in order and my credit number remains in the low 800's. My home is a little showplace and although I'm not a neat-freak, I don't like outward chaos to connect with the inward chaos I experience on a daily basis, so I keep a tidy house and fool everybody.

I have a Bachelor's degree that I never used.

I have a Master's degree that I never used.

Some of my friends think I'm *beautiful* and others use the word *attractive*. Somebody once used the word *handsome* but they're dead now.

What I do have is beautiful hair. That's like saying someone has a great personality; it's what they don't say that really matters. But people have stopped me on the street and told me this. Unfortunately, it's always women who stop me.

I have very few phobias. The fact that I won't travel more than fifty miles from home, and only in clear weather, and never at night, is a moot point. That would help make me a cheap date and a cheaper wife. Big trips for me would be going to the mall in the next county over.

So when I applied for this dating service, I filled out the forms, stated the obvious and unleashed my soul. One man dared to step out and communicate with me through a hidden e-mail connection. We exchanged about a half dozen blurbs and I never heard from him again. I just don't understand men. I didn't make that big a deal out of the toe.

These things simply don't work like the ads tell you they will. I'm sure it has something to do with being older or else it's simply that all the good men don't have internet access.

Or it just might not be the Lord.

(Please note: I did not really talk about that toe, and half of what I said here in this vignette is a fabrication. It was inserted for its humor—for some necessary comic relief.)

Rental Case

I rented out my home for a full school year and attended a Spirit-filled Bible college about an hour's drive away. I lived on the campus. It was nice to find a place where I was allowed to scream and cry at high pitch and no one would call the police. They would, however, pray in tongues, take authority over demons, and hope the semester would come to an end quickly.

My intentions were to get away to a safe place and hoped

the college community would, before the end of the school year, take me in on a permanent basis. Neither intention was met.

The experience did, however, leave me with two lasting friendships and a good, old-fashioned horror story.

Early on, during that first semester, I was doing nothing more than walking through a parking lot to get to a class, when a man approached me asking directions to a particular building. No one comes to this place without knowing what it is—a Bible college—and our conversation easily led to the Lord. We shared our faith for a few moments and made the mistake of exchanging names. When he heard mine, his face contorted into a frenzied look, his eyes darted back and forth and his voice screeched as he cried out, "So YOU'RE that evil woman I heard about! How dare you come against a man of God like that? "

I later learned he was mentally ill, off his meds, and on the loose.

I nearly joined him.

So Long, Solo

I've been on my own now for several years and have griped to the Lord about it too many times to count. If He knows how many hairs are on my head, He's able to give me that exact number, too, but I'm not interested in a number count. I'm interested in getting an answer to my prayer, or my gripe, however it's labeled. I prefer to look at my communication with the Lord as prayers, a kind of Psalms of Carol, a little bit of "How long, Oh, Lord?"

Just because my age starts with a 6 doesn't make me exempt from sounding like those of you with a 2 or 3 in front of yours.

I think I despise singleness, which is not good. In glancing through my writings and journals, I can see where my desperation began to replace my dependence on God. I sounded fairly sincere until I attached a little pinch of panic or control into the mix.

2009

I despise how I live. (Oops, **that's** where that word came from.)

Alone.

Okay, that's not exactly living victoriously for the Lord, now is it? But I got so used to being married. I'm convinced I like the idea of marriage a lot more than marriage itself. Truth is, I love having a companion; someone to talk to and plan with. It's motivating. No one in my home is suggesting I do something other than my own self, and self-motivator is not a word anyone would use to define my personality. So this means I'm stuck. I can't move because I don't know what the direction forward might be exactly.

You told me You would be my husband. I'm not exactly crazy about that idea anymore. Talk to me.

2010

This is what I see in myself—a caring and tender-hearted human being who has been without any form of reciprocation of that caring and tenderness for years now and it has brought me to a place of desperation and longing that is both painful and harmful for me on a spiritual level. My thoughts have been so wrong; my affections have been in the wrong place and for this, Lord, I ask You to cleanse me and forgive me. Allow me to move forward with this experience serving only to strengthen the person I am within and lead me, I pray, to the man who is just right for all my needs.

Sooner rather than later, please.

2012

Apparently someone got in the habit of hanging a pair of blue jeans in the size their ideal husband would wear on one of the four posters of their bed-frame. Every night, the woman would point to the jeans and pray aloud, "Lord, fill 'em."

My guestroom bed has four posters on it and I seriously thought of exchanging my own bedroom set with that one for, well, what I just said. I said seriously thought. Seriously.

I keep seeing an image of Jesus and He is sitting on a park bench. His head is in His hands and it is bent down into His chest. His shoulders are wiggling up and down. He is laughing. He is laughing about this. He is laughing with me.

But I really mean it. "Fill 'em, Lord."

2013

There is one huge advantage to being single and alone. I have complete control of the remote. This is lame, I know, but I was told to look on the bright side of being single and that's all I've been able to come up with so far.

When I finally open up my heart to the husband He is to me, I hear His words far better and I begin to see and understand

what He has been rescuing me from and where He is taking me. I'm not much of a traveler, but at least with Him, we're getting somewhere and He 's a really good driver.

Chapter Ten

Save For The Spirit of Truth

Poison Control

Some poisons take awhile to take effect. They have to be dispersed over a period of time, usually in tiny doses and subtly. Always subtly. You're not supposed to be able to tell if a food or a drink has a slight, say, almond taste to it. Or maybe it tastes a lot like Kool-Aid. You just take what you're served and you trust it to provide the nourishment you need or the quench to your thirst. After time, it builds up and begins the steady process of destruction. Its final end, left untreated, is death.

It's a lot like the frog-in-the-pot story. Put a frog in a pot of boiling water and he'll leap out of that thing faster than his tongue laps a fly out of the air. Put him in a pan of cool water and he'll sit tight and never notice when the heat's been turned up gradually until he becomes the meat for the stew.

Either way, in either story, you're going to die if you don't put a halt to what's about to kill you. The key to your escape is recognizing you're smack dab in the middle of being destroyed and you need to end it before it ends you. C. S. Lewis says in *Screwtape Letters*, "The safest road to Hell is the gradual one— the gentle slope, soft underfoot, without sudden turnings, without milestones, without... signposts." What keeps you from recognizing what is happening to you is called deception. It's the enemy's biggest ploy and it always comes disguised. It has to: you're not supposed to know it's there and you'll never know it's there until you recognize it. It's a Catch-22.

And it's the basis of every horror story on the silver screen.

Save for the Spirit of Truth.

Defining Deception

Deception, officially speaking, is the practice of deliberately making somebody believe things that are not true, a kind of trick or strategy intended to mislead somebody. That said, it is important to state that most people are not deceivers in and of themselves.

But all the devils in hell *are*. Separating the devils from the devilish is one thing. Separating them from how they play into the life of my brothers and sisters in Christ is quite another.

TD Jakes put it this way: "Many times people don't (hurt/mislead/criticize) you because they are evil; they do it because they've been trained to think anyone who doesn't perceive and see things in the same manner is an enemy."*

If someone is deceiving someone else, chances are fairly good the deceived party is not aware of what is taking place. And there's also a good chance that the one doing the deceiving could also be unaware of his or her own deception. It depends, I believe, on where they're getting their training. The sad rule is this: *you don't know you're living in deception until you are out of it.* The other option is that it has taken over you. Frog soup.

I wish there was another way to get that revelation but I haven't discovered it yet. It takes a miracle of God and maybe also someone praying for you.

In order to realize you are suddenly free from it, you need hindsight. If you stay in your deception, you may never grasp the pure definition of deception. You might actually be entombed in it and your perceived definition of deception is, in reality, actually deceiving you.

Save for the Spirit of Truth.

* From a Google + post, Jan. 5, 2013

Beauty Or The Beast

The Lord used *fish*, of all things, to give me spiritual insight into deception. That He speaks to us through creation and the laws of nature is a given. For example, you only have to know that pearls develop through irritation and diamonds through heat and pressure to get an inkling of the ways of the Lord in His dealings with His children. We don't become jewels overnight or without a struggle.

I was visiting Sea World in Orlando, Florida, stuck in its main building because of a violent lightening storm raising havoc on the sidewalks outside. To occupy myself, I took the time to read the small print next to each exhibit I'd previously just strolled by. It was then I was reintroduced to two particular fish with the title—Most Poisonous Fish in the Ocean.

The most dangerous fish is called a Stone Fish; they blend into their environment and resemble the very rocks they settle on. How they got their name is a no-brainer. The other is known as

the Turkey Fish and comes in a close second in the poisonous department. Turkey Fish, incredibly stunning in appearance, are not scared of anything because they have no predators; the poison of other dangerous fish has no affect on them. What draws in their prey is their beauty.

One is camouflaged, rather ugly and almost invisible while the other is alluring, attractive, and distracting. Their drawing powers seem in direct opposition to each other and that might just be the point. What works for one might not work for the other. Whatever the method, both have the power to draw in a gullible population. Their final goal is to conquer, capture, and destroy.

Little devils with fins.
So it is with deception:
Save for the Spirit of Truth.

In The Be-Ginning

Take, for instance, the story of Adam and Eve and the first sin. We all tend to think Eve is the real culprit here until we fine-tune the story and get a richer perceptive of what happened in the Garden. Adam and Eve had a great thing going until the serpent came up with a plan to deceive them. God told Adam not to eat of the fruit of that one, single tree, The Tree of the Knowledge of Good and Evil. Everything else was up for grabs.

The devil pulls a good one—he quotes the rules exactly—

but he questions the one restriction itself by stating, "Has God indeed said?"

We have to remember that Eve wasn't around when the ground rules were laid.

So when the enemy questioned the Word of God to Eve, her response might have been taken from what she had been told by Adam. There is nothing in Genesis 2 or 3 to suggest God had a separate conversation with Eve about the rules or that Adam passed the word on to her in error. Nor is there anything written to imply that Eve embellished what she heard Adam tell her; it just shows us that she did. We are told her response to the serpent was, *"We may eat of the fruit of the trees of the garden; but of the fruit of the tree which is in the midst of the garden, God has said, 'You shall not eat it, nor shall you touch it, lest you die.'"*

Eve's response to the rule was to add to the rule, to add to the law, to, shall we say, get *religious or legalistic* about it. She said God said not to eat or touch the fruit. Well, that's not what He said. He only said not to eat from the tree. He didn't say anything about touching it.

Either way and anyway, this is very simply "adding to the law."

Legalism made its grand entrance very early on, and attached itself to deception and sin. It is an oh-so-subtle act we might not easily see. And that is its intention. That is deception, and it plays into everything that is not God.

That first act of disobedience indicates Adam was standing right there next to Eve and, apparently, not saying or doing a thing. Was he curious to see what would happen? Was he supposed to step in and protect the woman? Who is really at

fault here, we argue? There are certainly a lot of what-if's and superfluous innuendoes hanging in the air on the male/female wrongdoer. I tend to think there's a higher power at work here making the blame-game a waste of time.

Sin, just simply said, is not gender-biased.

What we really need to see (have we perhaps been deceived about this?) is how subtly we embellish the truth, under the guise of doing good. We are simply doing more than is required or expected, and herein lies the problem with the law of the past battling within us to override the grace of the present—the here and now—that the Gospel brings.

Save for the Spirit of Truth.

Getting Unhooked

Right after the terrible tragedy at the Sandy Hook school, conspiracy theories were on the web faster than you can say Facebook. They were eye-opening, jaw-dropping and convincing to a fault. I got confused and practically convinced myself it was indeed a government-based plot to control munitions before I realized, once again, you can turn and twist everything around and make it work for you. Acclaimed atheists do it all the time with the Bible, and the media is usually their vehicle of choice. If there is an agenda to fill, a goal to reach, a people to hoodwink, that's the way to do it. Get someone to question truth by taking them on a never-ending bunny trail, or twisting the truth just a fraction. Get them to see another side, another angle. Don't let anyone see what's really going on here.

Just saying—it's easy, too easy, to become trapped by a tiny twist or a little addition.

Save, of course, for the Spirit of Truth.

In Defence Of

I need to attach a warning label here. Loving Jesus is not hazardous to your health; it is vitally and eternally beneficial to it. What is hazardous is the misunderstanding and/or the tainting of His message.

The church I was in did wonderful things, on so many levels. The relationships were there, the visiting ministers and Bible scholars were a blessing, the times spent in prayer and praise and prophetic anointing existed, the outreaches made to the community were undeniable, and there was a sincere burden felt for souls to be saved. Hundreds, maybe even thousands of people were led to the Lord, or changed by a revelation, or helped in some way.

I cannot, nor will not, compare my old church to the Latter Day Saints or Hari Krishnas, nor the pastors and my husband to the likes of Jim Jones or David Koresh. That would be wrong, untrue, highly foolish, completely unfair, downright stupid, and actually evil. It would also be a judgment and that's the kind of thing I'm learning to avoid. But we are told to discern the spirits and something was *off*. Something that is *off*, even just a fraction,

can become the starting place for cults. It is a lot like, as my Dad used to say, being just a little bit pregnant or having a little bit of cancer. Something has begun and it has to grow. That's the way both are designed. In the end, its fruition brings either life or death. You must learn how to recognize the difference and that is not always an easy thing to do.

Save for the Spirit of Truth.

Traditions Of Men

My old church family/leaders were only doing what they were told to do. The problem was it wasn't Biblical instructions they were following on how you "run a church," especially in how you deal with specks in people's eyes. Somebody added to the law a long time ago and I guess nobody, or so I thought, questioned it. Our leaders were all trained from within.

I have since learned that many others in the church did question certain beliefs and policies throughout the years and, when they did, were rebuked and returned sheepishly to the fold. They repented and submitted; or else they left the church completely, and always in disgrace. We made sure they left that way.

I was always told, "They couldn't handle the dealings of the Lord." or "Our vision is something they aren't strong enough or willing enough to enter into."

No question, I would have stayed within the framework of this mind-set, save for the Spirit of Truth.

Chapter Eleven
STRUGGLING

Ifs Ands And Buts

If things have changed back at my old church...

If there are no longer control issues in the leadership

If rules and regulations and sin-snooping is obsolete

If I wouldn't recognize the place were I to sneak into it (wearing a disguise, of course)

Then I would say, "Good. Very good. "

And if timing is everything, I would say I was there at the wrong time—when things were not good and grace was assigned the wrong definition.

Because—I want to believe—both of us are growing and both of us are changing. That's what healthy bodies are supposed to do.

Then, I have one last question:

But isn't an apology in order?

Hurt People Hurt People

But what if the person who is doing the hurting is the pastor and what if the person he is hurting is his wife? And what if the pastor trains his elders who are also hurting and they counsel all the hurting people in the church?

In such a case, people are going to get hurt and maybe people are not going to get well.

I knew my husband was still hurting from his first marriage. His first wife unexpectedly and painfully betrayed him big time. I've spoken with his first wife and she verified this to me. I don't believe you can just get past betrayal by training yourself to look good. Hurts like this have a deeper root system and pretending you are fine when you are not is like weeding the garden by mowing the lawn or like rearranging the furniture to hide that stain on the rug.

He shared what happened in his first marriage just one time with the congregation, decades ago, but acknowledging it to them didn't make the mess go away. He kept saying he was fine and I was the one who was the problem. So I continued trying to live with the mess it left and now he has two ex-wives.

It hurts me to know that.

We Were All In The Bus Crash

I have likened our divorce and what occurred in our church afterwards to a bus crashing through a guardrail and hurtling down a steep embankment. A crash like that leaves multiple, wounded people scattered in various directions, in desperate need of help and healing. The severity of the injuries depend on how close the person was sitting to the point of impact or whether or not they were thrown out of the bus, or maybe even under it. I'm pretty sure that what happened to me sitting right at the impact point was all of the above.

Anyone who works as a medic will tell you triage might not always be effective in identifying internal wounds. Measuring a person's outward appearance can mask serious injury that assuredly will, in time, rise to the surface, injuries that might even prove to be life-threatening.

Many are placed in the ICU, often clinging to life for long periods of time. These gravely wounded patients are in no physical, emotional or spiritual position to help anyone else during their recovery. They're forced to deal with their own injuries and their own healing process, and the length of time it takes depends on the severity of their wounds. Some wounds are compounded by previous trauma; some patients are fragile to begin with, intensifying the severity of the new injuries.

Knowing this helps me better understand the bigger picture, concerning my own recovery and those of my fellow passengers. We all crashed, we all rolled down the hill, and we're all struggling to get back *there*.

And the sad truth is that some never survived the crash.

As I See It

I recall squirming just a bit when someone told a true story about themselves and followed it with the statement,

"At least that's the truth, as I see it."

You mean to tell me there is more than one truth? That there is something more than just "the way I see it" and "the other side of the story"?

That's not what I learned in Sunday School.

Does that mean that if I tell someone about something that happened to me that is true, it is really only the way in which I perceived it and it may very well be a total opposite of what it is that really happened? Or is it something like peering into the peepholes of a circus fence and seeing an elephant from varying angles and degrees?

If I tell you I see a huge ear and you tell me "no, it is not anything like an ear; it is a long tube with two holes that look like large nasal passages at the end," am I lying?

Those, and other stupid thoughts, make war inside my head, but I can only tell you my story, as I see it. It is a lot like the injured person who remembers nothing about the bus accident or the driver or the other passengers or the circumstances that led to the accident. He just knows he ended up in the ICU with massive injuries and a number of witnesses told him what they saw from where they stood.

At their angle.

To their degree.

Through their assigned peephole.

Maybe even from another ICU.

So we all were in this horrible crash and I can only tell you where **I** hurt.

A Heavy Word

I read something by Philip Yancey, the man who is probably my favorite author. He was speaking about the perils of being a writer and most especially a Christian writer. As writers, we have to stick to the naked word because we're not there in public, using our facial expressions to communicate more than our words can, nor are we there to play on emotions to get someone to agree with us. Because of that, we can't even determine how what we write will be received. He spoke of a time when he mentioned a Christian friend in one of his writings, a man who battled a lot more in life than most people. The man he wrote about said he felt as if he was reduced to a two paragraph illustration rather than someone who was following God and trying so hard to be a real person.

I don't want to make that mistake but am realizing I can't avoid it. The heaviness of the responsibility that will follow the telling of this story has been weighing upon me.

I think this is my reality check.

I've lived in a constant but healthy fear of screwing up what I believe I need to say in telling my story. I admit to exposing people's faults and frailties, my own included, sins that should have been forgiven and secrets that should have been forgotten. To be perfectly honest, I have not revealed all of the story or the worst of the story. Those parts are the ones that will remain in my Ponder Pocket. I've worked through a lot of pain and bad attitudes and have altered my intention for wanting others to know what happened from my end of the bus crash about a half dozen times.

"*Lord,*" I said, "*what if they take what I wrote the wrong way? What if they don't see my growth or my heart and misconstrue my intentions or my objectives?*"

That's the way you think when you care, and it's also the way you think when you have an inordinate desire to want everybody to love you.

"*Carol,*" He told me, "*you should see what they did with MY book. You should hear what they thought I was saying. You'd be amazed at how they turned my objectives around. You've had only a taste of it. I drank the whole cup. Share what you know and let Me take care of what happens next.*"

Then I remembered He cares too; that He wishes everybody would love Him as well. I'm the one who gets inordinate about it.

He's the One who has it all under control.

Still Struggling

I'm a big baby when it comes to verbal assaults. I also cringe at the idea that some people continue to claim I lost my mind and was (or still am) demon possessed. It breaks my heart to realize I may get some hate mail amidst a lot of thank you notes, so I want to get the point across that:

1) This book is how I view what happened to me and what I am to learn from it, and I believe it is the Lord who is showing me these things.

2) I admit to not having the whole picture (that elephant through the fence thing).

3) I absolutely never ever meant to hurt anybody ever, and especially not through writing this book.

A friend of mine, a Christian counselor by profession, lovingly said to me, "It sounds like you are saying you will need to pass things by other people for the rest of your life to make sure you are not in the wrong."

She's right. That is *exactly* how I feel...so afraid of making a mistake—of upsetting others and making God look bad. I am, admittedly, just trying to tell the truth in the kindest way possible. Truth is easier to iron out than an intentional lie. I want to speak the truth but I still need to remember this is about my family as well as my church family. If the Lord is going to have me be this bold, can I maintain my composure and stay strong

in what I have disclosed?   There is a part of me that knows my own healing from legalism is found in facing what follows and trusting Him in it.

It is the prophetess thing, I have concluded. I must say what I sense the Lord is telling me to say and leave it alone and take what comes. For me, that is the most difficult part of all. I don't like having stones thrown at me. Sticks and stones may break my bones, but words will rip my guts apart.

I think, Lord, this is where You come in. You've been there. You've done that.

So, people, you can call me crazy, if you must. He took it and He'll show me how to, also. Just don't put a pea under my mattress.

The Word Made Flesh

I've been handed a gift. It is to write. It is also a back-hoe, a power saw, and a stick of dynamite. If I am going to use words, I have to understand what it is these words hold, for me as well as for the readers. There is a lot of energy emitting from just 26 little letters.

From the very beginning, God Himself merely had to say, "Let there be…" and it became whatever it was He said: light, land, water, herb, fruit, and tree. Then He made man and woman in His image and He gave them the power to re-create, both with words and with loins. Since I never birthed a baby, I suppose I get my fix from birthing stories and pray there is life at the end.

It makes no difference that I am not birthing a "real" life because there are still labor pains felt in the process and, in a sense, can be equally as excruciating.

Especially because I have lived the very words I'm using. They are not figments of my imagination. And because I have lived them and am sharing them, I have to remind myself I am operating a backhoe, working with a power saw, holding a stick of dynamite.

John 1:1 says, "In the beginning was the Word and the Word was with God and the Word was God." Verse 14 tells us "And the Word became flesh and dwelt among us..." He spoke Himself into existence. There is a great responsibility that comes with being made in His image. There is something profound He is revealing to us about creation and image and self.

The God I have come to know is super-picky about making sure we *live* a thing, that we *know* a thing, that we *experience* a thing before we really have the right to speak *anything* into anyone else's life. This is the place where my confidence comes from. In living out these last few years, I can only tell it as it is and believe the words are honing in on all the right places and in all the hurting hearts—digging up, slicing up, and blowing up all the junk that gets in the way of truly knowing and loving the Lord.

In some weird sort of way, it might actually be more intense than what a woman experiences from her time of transition to birth. But what do I know? I've only birthed a book. I did, however, scream a lot getting there.

Snippets

I was on a roller coaster ride with my emotions during this time, this awful journey. I found myself weighing what my heart was knowing with what my mind and emotions were telling me. They were not in agreement and they were, for lack of a better term, whack-a-doodle. To read my journal entries is to read into the thought life of the double-minded man. I went back and forth and up and down and in and out. The Lord allowed me to spew, to rant, to holler, to cry, to scream, to shout, to pray, to sing, to talk, to screech, to communicate on every level. I know I hated it then and I know now He embraced and held me the whole time. That's what He does. That's what He's there for.

Ranting

As of this moment in time I continue to carry the stigma that comes with being a divorcee and the several hundred people who once went to the church my ex-husband and I pastored still will have nothing to do with me and I am still estranged from some family members and my only child, a single mom, continues to blame me for the destruction of the family unit which includes both our immediate family and the church family. Yes, I know, that is a run-on sentence. But so is my life and there has been no pause, no break from the mayhem that ensued at the time of the bus crash.

Excuse me (and please forgive me) while I rant a little. To everyone, and you know who you are, who stopped talking to me: Why did you all desert me and call me a liar when all I could do was assume, based on what I heard through the grapevine? You were talking about me but no one was talking to me, so what else could I do? What's wrong with you guys, anyway? Did you take off your WWJD* bracelets or something?

Okay, I feel better now.

I have had done to me what I never thought would happen. I know I love the Lord and yet I have been abandoned and disfellowshipped. Oops, Microsoft Word doesn't recognize that word, disfellowshipped.

Neither, it seems, does Jesus.

When all of this happened, the Lord told me I was "blameless and innocent" concerning what happened.

So why doesn't anybody else know that?

I realize you were ignorant and I can forgive you for that. But I'm still working on the forgiveness part with those closest to me, and I haven't been able to totally do that yet. I'm not Jesus, but I do want to be like Him. That should count for something. That should set me on the right path to getting there.

* What would Jesus do?

No More Ranting

My original intention was to broadcast all the horrible things that were done to me and, in the telling, make a whole lot of people look bad. It didn't take long to realize a whole lot of people were going to discover it was me who looked bad.

Blame will do that.

217

Sometimes you can be a good example and sometimes you can be a good example of what not to do. Be careful, Carol, when you *Show and Tell*.

Right after our divorce, a man who had only been a Christian a few months, told his friend he was going to get a divorce, too. If it was okay for a pastor to do it, it would be more than okay for him. Case in point.

Confession

I have now seen what I was like just before you all turned your back on me and I admit, I'd be frustrated with me, too.

People have told me I am such a strong woman. No, I am a loud woman.

Truth

It's called Friendly Fire. It's when someone in the military service of their country, accidentally shoots and injures, or kills, one of its own. It's bad enough to be injured, worse to die, and heartbreaking beyond words because it's an accident. I attribute what happened to me to be Friendly Fire. I don't believe the people I loved for decades ever meant to release their ammunition at my heart with the intention of destroying me as a person. Yet that is what happened, in a sense, with the events surrounding the bus crash.

What made it all the more painful in the recovery was realizing the ones who fired the shots didn't even know shots were fired.

Deception and Control

"There's a core of truth to every good lie." I heard that on a television show. I know it works because I learned it the hard way. It's the key ingredient to making frog soup.

There's a reason God argued with His people and tried to talk them out of asking for a leader. We often end up putting the crown on the wrong king.

I will make only one mention of anything political. I'm not politically bent nor am I politically savvy. I do, however, keep up with the news and have a brain that works well enough to tell me something is happening. The way the church goes, so, I suspect, goes the government. If you are adding new rules for your people to follow, if you are allowing yourself too much control, if you are making frog soup—you might be a pastor or a politician.

Religion and Legalism

Every story about the religious Pharisees, the same ones Jesus rebuked, seems to have a common theme: nitpicking on what is not important. I heard a story of a man held up by a thief. When the thief realized he was holding up a Catholic priest, he stopped and apologized. The priest offered the thief a candy bar and he replied, *"No thanks, I gave up candy for lent."*
That's what I'm talking about.

The church wounds its wounded and calls it ministry.
Religion labels any woman who is outspoken or disagrees

with leadership, a Jezebel. I have learned that a Jezebel isn't a controlling woman—it is a controlling spirit with a religious face—a face that is neither male nor female.

I would easily say "religion" doesn't just wound. It has the capacity to kill. It has already killed. I can back it up with Scripture: *"The letter kills but the spirit gives life"* (2 Corinthians 3:6).

Apparently, I've had the whole alphabet poured over my head.

Yes, I firmly believe Legalism kills. I've seen dozens of bruised and battered sheep all over the hillsides and some of them are mortally wounded. You can't help the mortally wounded, but you can triage the rest of the hill and do whatever you can to pour in the oil and the wine.

Healing

They said I lied, they said I was crazy, they said I didn't hear from the Lord and that I certainly wasn't following Him. I didn't lie, I almost went crazy, but I knew exactly Who it was I was following. I just wasn't all too fond, initially, of where He was taking me.

If there was a sign-up sheet for this kind of life, I certainly don't remember being stupid enough to sign it. But I did sign it, April 22, 1973 at two o'clock in the morning.

I have been shown that life can sometimes be bad but You

are always good, that it is better to be real than to be religious, that walking with You will always lead to the Cross and that there really is no plan B.

"Lord, how come you have used the people I tend to want to hate to get me healed?"

"It was through people I could have hated that the stripes were inflicted that heal you."

It's okay to be bummed; just make sure you follow it up with surrender. Even Jesus didn't want the cup right away.

"I think I might be too hurt to heal." I said that once, and got rebuked. Not by people.

We might actually be a victim when we don't know the Lord, but when we do, we can no longer use victim as an excuse not to heal. We become recipients of grace and the one real victim, Jesus.

I was once asked if I had any regrets in my life. I distinctly remember responding that I had none. I had learned many valuable lessons from what could have been deep regrets. I also indicated I was living a perfect and fulfilling life and wouldn't change a thing.

That was before the bus crash.

Someone recently asked me the same question. I'm still

working on the answer, certain there **will** be an answer I can confidently come back with.

Dietrich Bonheoffer said, *"Silence in the face of evil is itself evil. Not to speak is to speak. Not to act is to act."* Yes, he was referring to the Nazis and he lost his life speaking out. But it's the part about not speaking that hurts so much. It was the choice my friends and family made regarding me. It kept me both in the dark and at bay, but as awful as it was, it led me into a much brighter place and a clearer understanding of grace.

There is nothing at all evil about embracing grace, especially when there is nothing else to hold on to. Grace brings healing.

It's important to remember that most people come into the Kingdom with more luggage than a world leader's daughter traveling with her security detail. That's when we call luggage, baggage. We need to remind them on a regular basis that the Bellboy is fully aware of His job: He will carry it for us; He isn't intimidated by our "security requirements;" and He doesn't require a tip.

Please, church, allow me the grace to get healthier, the time to work through things, to walk out the business of processing who God is in the light of what I have just been through. I've seen some pretty unattractive body parts in the Body of Christ and refuse to believe God is anything like man when man gets religious.

Let me learn to find answers for myself and to allow healing as it comes and don't don't don't tell me what God doesn't like about me until after He's told me Himself.

Just As I Am

I now attend a home church where I can be accepted, as the song goes, *just as I am.* I think that song should apply well past its calling to the altar for salvation; it should be ongoing throughout an entire lifetime spent walking with Christ.

Thankful

During those early years in the desert, I have no memory whatsoever about where I spent my holidays. I only know it was with people who were not my family and were not at all familiar. Thank you, whoever you are. The days were a blur but your kindness was clear; it helped me heal.

Purpose

Sometimes I wonder which body part I am. Then I remember, no matter the part, I am forever, and rather firmly, attached to all those other parts, even the ones who drive me crazy or hurt me to the max.

I think what made me saddest of all, once left to fend for myself, was not just the absence of people but the absence of purpose. They left together, intertwined.

In my search for purpose, I asked the Lord to give me a

four-word ministry, one that breaks the yoke in just four little words, just like the lady in the kitchen's four words did for me when she said, "It's not your fault."

But all He said was, *"**Go** forward."*

He is so witty.

EVEN THOUGH.......I WILL FOLLOW YOU

Even though not all inside Your doors
    have pure hearts;
Even though not all in the chairs
    have souls truly sincere;
Even though from up front can come lies and serious errors
    wounding many;
Yet, I will continue to follow You, Lord.

Even though some leaders of Your flock
    are wolves under cover;
Even though hunger for attention drew some to the top
    instead of Your true call;
Even though they have led many to a stumbling block
    and I was one who fell;
Yet, You are the Light I want in my soul

Even though all the leaders are mere, faulty men
    who make many blunders;
Even though in their ignorance they
    can cause so much pain;
Even though when proven wrong
    few ever apologize;
Yet, in You I seek my refuge and song.

Even if all Your followers falter, including myself;
    You are worthy of my faith;
    You alone will never fail me;
    You will not let me be destroyed.
I will trust in You.
I will trust in You.

Cheryl Zehr, July 1997
(After an almost fatal church wounding)

Chapter Twelve

God provides

Unearthing Provision

I waited for the third appliance to show some signs of premature death. The hot water heater was making the same noises that I'm convinced have been used in torture treatments. The refrigerator was spewing out enough energy to double my monthly electric bill. I knew these things came in threes so I waited for the third appliance to do something creative, like flood a room or start a fire. I was just entering the wilderness and I wasn't yet familiar with provision. Of course, I prayed. If I remember correctly, the prayer was interspersed with sobs and snot.

Instead, the doorbell rang and a strange man stood outside my door. He was wearing a hardhat and there was a utility truck in my neighbor's driveway. There was also a backhoe in the middle of my cul-de-sac and three or four men either walking down my driveway or standing on my lawn. I was never aware of the clatter or the commotion. The sounds that scream in your head are sometimes too loud making what is within hearing distance become white noise.

"Sorry to bother you, Ma'am, but half the electricity in your neighbors' house has gone out and we've traced it to a line buried under your front yard. We're going to have to dig up part of your yard and we might have to take out one or two of those fully-grown trees to get to it. We'll refill and reseed what we dig up and you'll be fully compensated for the going rate of the cost to replace those trees. I'm really sorry."

I'm really not sorry at all. The going rate exactly covered the cost of a new hot water heater and a refrigerator.

I never missed the trees; they only blocked my view of a world that lay just outside my door.

Turkey Fish

I was gullible, I was stupid, I was not thinking, and all of the above when I purchased that house in that senior housing division. It was at the time when the housing market was practically giving houses away and I thought I could handle "such a deal" and all that went into taking care of it. I let myself be duped by a sweet-talking, baby-faced contractor who had me convinced everything was aboveboard as he walked me through the process. He lied to my face, schemed behind my back, broke the law on more than one occasion, and led me into a contract I couldn't get out of in any legal way. And, toward the end, he got real mean.

He was a Turkey Fish.

I repented.

I was forced to close on the house, anyway.

A few days later, the school tax bill arrived in the mail and it was more than one-third my yearly income.

I repented again.

The following week, I was driving home from church and mentally devising a new way to repent that might bring about a miracle, when I noticed a house for sale four doors away from mine. An Open House allowed me to go into the place and scout out the market. I absolutely had to sell my house before my credit score took a nosedive in direct relation to not paying that school tax bill. It was not a seller's market and I was painfully aware of that.

As I walked down the driveway to the front door, I met a couple about my age walking out of the house and I casually asked them, "How did you like the house?"

"It's too small for what we're looking for," the woman replied.

"Want to come and see mine?" I responded. "It's for sale, too, and it's a lot bigger."

Now, I'm not sure that's what I said. I don't remember deciding to be so bold, and it certainly wasn't my intention to talk to complete strangers that way. Still, I must have said something somewhat similar to that because they followed me back to my house and purchased it with a cash offer; an offer $17,000 more than what I had just paid for it the week before.

Turkey Fish might be immune to the poison of others, but they don't know a Savior who forgives our sins, a God who answers our prayers, a Father who restores what is lost, or a Husband who provides what is needed.

Or, as I see it, a miracle-worker.

Song Choice

The song was in my head, first thing in the morning. It wouldn't go away and it made no sense to sing it. I actually found it terribly irritating because it was so loud and clear and I assumed I ought to be carrying around something far more spiritual in my thoughts, like an old hymn or a new Hillsong release. I rebuked the devil but the song continued.

I hate it when that happens.

The itsy bitsy spider went up the water spout.
Down came the rain and washed the spider out.
Out came the sun and dried up all the rain,
And the itsy bitsy spider went up the spout again.

I was about to invest nearly every dollar I owned in a reverse mortgage enterprise. It meant I'd lose all my money and have to live in this house until I was dragged out screaming or carried out in silence, under an off-white sheet. There was more than lack of money at stake here; there was this trust-issue-thingy. This was the Lord's choice for me, and He was telling me to trust Him for all my needs all my life.

The reverse mortgage was a decision I was forced to make when jobs didn't come, I didn't win any of the HGTV contests I entered, and nobody remembered me in their will. It was the only choice left for me, outside of subsidized housing or a double-wide trailer. I went to embark on both alternatives and heard a very clear, *"No, I have another plan for you."*

His plan was this reverse mortgage thing. My choice was I

could live by the skin of my teeth and be miserable, or I could trust in God and be blown away by the One who promised to be my husband/provider. The reverse mortgage door was opened to me through the government HUD program and it seemed the sensible and the right answer to my housing needs—but scary.

That trust-issue-thingy kept coming up.

Getting a good night's sleep, on the other hand, didn't. I was worrying, afraid to go through with it. I found myself tossing and turning on the couch every other night. (I was avoiding my bed and my bedroom, a place that now seemed like enemy territory.) All this restlessness was doing its job—tormenting me to the point that I could actually feel my blood pressure rising and the lack of sleep taking its mental toll.

This inability to trust the Lord to work things out for me and meet my daily needs was not a new occurrence, nor was it limited to only my life. I re-read some of the Psalms, had a good, long talk with the Lord, and felt a little better. I became convinced that David might have actually had something similar to PMS when he wrote some of those Psalms. We connected in a weird sort of way.

And then this stupid song got stuck in my head and it wouldn't go away.

Hours into the day, and tons of prayer later, the song remained and I had to deduce it must be from the Lord. Once I accepted that, it wasn't long before I heard His voice.

"You're the spider."

The itsy bitsy spider went up the water spout.

Okay, Father, so I'm pretty small. I already know that. And I'm going up the water spout. That sounds a lot like me, all right.

I am daily going to the source of where that Living Water resides and drinking from it so that I might survive.

I continued with something like, *"That's cute, but aren't we getting a little bit too spiritually-minded here?"*

I've learned it's okay to talk to Him like that. He gets me.

Down came the rain and washed the spider out.

It's a funny thing about water. We need it to survive but too much of it can drown us. I knew enough about what religiosity does to people to know that too much of it can destroy the simplicity of Christianity. The song was taking on a more meaningful stance, and I was pretty confident that its author had absolutely no spiritual objective when it was written.

Out came the sun and dried up all the rain,

Okay, I'm catching on, I think. How do you spell SON, anyway?

And the itsy bitsy spider went up the spout again.

In spite of the opposition, that little critter continued the journey anyway, knowing exactly where provision was coming from.

HUD had just mailed me the last of my paperwork. Where do I sign?

Ten-Fold

I don't give to get back. Oh, okay, it's there in the back of my mind, but it's really not my first intention in the giving.

All of my giving, up to this point, is in the hearing and I heard something I did not like. I heard the Lord tell me to give a Christian television network $1,000.

First of all, I did not watch the station incessantly. I watched it occasionally and less and less. I was a graduate student (with funds from a fellowship the Lord had already provided*) and TV had turned into a reward system: finish your homework and you get to watch it. But this particular day, one of my favorite preachers was delivering a message that made me do that Amen thing, out loud, over and over. When I heard the Lord speak to me about giving that much money, I rebuked the devil and set it aside. It was a third of my savings. It had to be the devil.

The thought remained persistent and seemed to increase in volume, so I threw out a fleece. I came out with a three-fold criteria: the preacher had to say three specific things in his sermon, and I listed each one and presented it to the Lord. In less than ten minutes, all three of my conditions were met and I wrote out and mailed the $1,000 check.

A few months later, the head of the Scholarship Department from my college discovered a $10,000 scholarship that had been buried somewhere in their files and forgotten. Apparently, I met each of the three conditions for it and it was promptly added to my bank account.

I went out and bought a flat-screen.

*Details on how He provided this later.

What's Up, Chuck?

When the bus accident happened, nobody knew what to do with me so they did nothing. When you do nothing, you have really done something and so you **did** know what to do. I have finally concluded, nothing is paramount to abandonment. In actuality, doing nothing IS abandonment. It just has an excuse attached to it.

I had forgotten that a lot of us were on the same bus and might also still be in their own kind of ICU, fighting for their own lives, and unable to help anyone else recover. Still I thought it odd that not even one minister of the Gospel ever called or visited. Excommunication is just that—X.

The one woman from my old church who visited me regularly at first turned out to be a mole and, as I told you, reported everything I said to the pastors. But later there were others, outside my old church, who came to my aid and we always seemed to meet over a dinner plate.

The first couple to approach me was Bill and Sandy and they didn't give a hoot about what anyone else thought. They were in their late fifties, had no children of their own and doted on cats. They had a reputation for belonging to every Christian church in the area at one time or another and in the past, I had shrugged them off and given them a label. The fact that they were kind and sincere people went unnoticed. I was trained to zero in on their sin and I trained well.

They were the only couple to reach out to me for the better part of a year, and while they gave me fourteen hundred different reasons why they themselves had left my church some two decades before, they faithfully took me out to dinner once a week for several years. They let me verbally vomit on them at every meal and they vomited back on a consistent basis.

They had been hurt, too.

Another couple I knew from decades back heard about the bus crash and my weekly dinner sessions with Bill and Sandy and showed up to support me, embrace me, and regularly take me out to dinner another night of the week. They, too, had horror stories to tell about negative dealings with my church and its leadership and while the emotional support was helpful, the vomiting continued.

It seemed such a waste of many a good meal. But at least we all had something in common.

A few weeks later, Jake and Brenda congratulated me "for getting out from under," and began inviting me over for dinner and get-togethers centered on eating. They introduced me to Jim and Sally, who were still recovering from their own hellish nightmare in a church-related incident, and they introduced me to Steve and Ellen, who were licking their own wounds from a similar spiritually abusive situation and soon we were all sitting around and overeating and regurgitating on each other.

I believed I was, as the Scriptures say, *supping with the saints*.

I had just digested another full meal when I turned on the TV and listened to that screaming, southern preacher, the one I'm about to tell you about, who put it all into perspective for me—that regurgitating our troubles over and over is not a good thing and all the wrong doors get opened too many times. It simply doesn't lead to what has to be a necessary healing.

By then I had *supped* myself into a bad attitude and a size 14.

Party Invitation

Jesus asks the sick man what appears to be a stupid question: *"Do you want to be made well?"*

There is, of course, nothing stupid about what Jesus asks. Or does. Or says. It is stupid of us not to recognize that questions like this are looking for profound answers. We need to roll these kinds of questions around in our brain until the right answer comes and we need to reconsider what kind of answer Jesus might be searching for. He can be a trickster when it comes to these things.

I was asked that question once and didn't roll it around long enough when I quickly and religiously answered, *"Of course."*

Of course I lied. I didn't want to be well. I was having a great time celebrating my own pity party. Of course, I am the only one in the world who has ever done that.

The matre'd was formally attired in the standard black and white uniform, standing erect at the entrance to the sitting area, his arm placed firmly across his waist, a white, linen towel folded neatly over his forearm as he announced for all to hear:

"Pity party. Party of one."

It's perfectly human to wallow in self-pity, but only until you realize the Lord wants to deal with it. That's when we realize He isn't pitying with us—that He isn't pleased about our little party. Nobody, really, likes to dine alone.

Dealing with it has been the hardest thing I've ever done. Pity party aside, it has also been the *best* thing I've ever done.

Impregnated

The screaming southern preacher, who gave me the correct perspective about regurgitating, was having one big hallelujah session on Christian TV. I wasn't connecting with him as he carried his point and his voice to a higher place, but he was making mighty fine background noise. I figured, living alone, a good sermon might be the best kind of clamor to work its way around my house. I couldn't listen to Christian music anymore because those guttural, heaving kinds of sobs would start happening whenever I played a CD or tuned to Christian radio. I had to reduce my level of worship to just talk and the Lord seemed just fine with it. I didn't think it was really a reduction anyway; He knew I loved Him.

The particular sermon he was preaching was from Luke, about how Mary and Elizabeth got together for the first time after they both found out they were pregnant. I thought I knew the story but I didn't realize it held the key to what would become the measuring rod for everything I do and every choice I make.

"(Mary) entered the house of Zacharias and greeted Elizabeth. And it happened, when Elizabeth heard the greeting of Mary, that the babe leaped in her womb..."

Yeah, Lord, that's pretty cool.

I'd only been pregnant once and it only lasted a month. But I had a good idea how special that might have been for those cousins. But there was more to the story. There's always more to the story. Inspired by the concept the preacher was giving, I heard the Lord speaking directly to me.

"I want you to be careful, honey. I don't want you opening any door that doesn't make the life inside of you leap."

It was at this exact moment I was allowed to be "pregnant" again, with every intention of taking this one to full term.

Section Five

Break away

"...this is My Body, which is broken for you..."
I Cor. 11:24b

Chapter Thirteen

God restores

The Re Words

I started making a connection with the way in which all those *re* words pinpointed exactly what it was I was looking for—restoration, revival, redemption, repentance, respect, retribution, reaffirmation, reassurance, recognition, recompense, reconciliation. On its own, *re* means to bring back.

I made two honest attempts to be brought back into the fold.

The first time, I spoke with my Christian counselor, who was also a licensed mediator, and she agreed to help intervene on my behalf before the pastoral team. I was refused such a meeting on the grounds that my intentions were "questionable."

I never shared it with my counselor, but I knew one of those unwritten rules in our church was that Christian counselors were considered tainted by their worldly educational teachings and it was the ministry leaders who were more fitted by their position and their calling to handle situations that came up in the church dynamics. There might be true instances of this, but we were judging the majority of them as unfit.

The second time occurred when a pastor I never met, who lived in another state, heard about my situation and contacted me by e-mail. He listened to my story. He was the only minister to ask me to tell him what happened and after listening, expressed sympathy for my losses. He approached the pastoral team on my behalf and pleaded for our restoration.

He never got back to me after that encounter.

Waiting for him to call and share the outcome of their meeting became agonizing as I found myself longing, so to speak, to go back to Egypt and gnaw on a few leeks and garlic. I began calling this man over and over, for days on end, until he finally answered the phone. After much hemming and hawing, he related to me that he had learned from the pastors how evil I really was; so evil, he said, he would not even tell me what it was I had done to be labeled such a wicked person. It must have been even worse than what was written in that letter sent to the area churches early on, because none of those pastors reacted quite like this. He also told me I was never to darken the church doors again and that was the direct command of the pastors.

I think, though no one has ever told me directly, that might have meant I *was* excommunicated.

The *evil* part threw me for a loop. Would someone please give me some specifics on this topic and stop bantering that word around all the time? I still had no idea what I had done that would have the word *evil* attached to it.

This pastor said he was thoroughly rebuked for interfering in their church business and making contact with me. Of course I never heard from him again.

I saw that as sad. I saw the whole thing as sad. So I stayed that way for a long time. I stayed sad. No one from my old church but the mole came to visit. The divorce papers were the only thing to come in the mail. My daughter had a friend come and get her belongings. The only e-mails I received carried either strong rebukes or condemning accusations. The words in them were killing my soul. They had a life behind them that attached itself to the condemnation I was already trying to shed and I was gasping for every breath.

Family Re-Union

About two years later, one of the pastors from my old church asked an area minister to be a mediator for the two of us. It was his intention to begin the restoration process and this time it was his idea and not mine. This was because the pastor was my brother.

I suppose you can excommunicate a church member but you can't really excommunicate somebody in the family. Isn't blood, after all, supposed to be thicker than anything else?

The loss of my immediate family was, for me, a whole new and far deeper level of despair than anything else I had known following the bus crash. I was already missing out on all the events taking place within my church family. It was compounded by my daughter cutting me off for what amounted to five years, and by also being removed from all interaction with my own siblings and nieces and nephews. That included every holiday, every family reunion and every wedding I should have been invited to.

My response to the reconciliation invite surprised even me—I froze. I froze because my brother indicated he would begin the first order of business by presenting me with a list of all the grievances he had against me.

I was still in the early stages of rediscovering a God who had thrown sin into a sea of forgetfulness and was more concerned with moving forward. I was still learning how to release myself from the weight of carrying around a blame and shame that was never mine to carry. I was still trying to believe the sins I

245

was accused of committing were not sins at all. Yes, I had made mistakes and yes, I did and said a lot of stupid things in my life. But nothing I had said or done was worthy of the death penalty. That price got paid when Jesus died. Why would we even do that to each other?

The truth of the matter was in this one simple fact: Jesus Himself pulled me out of an unhealthy environment so I could get well. I didn't want to defend what He did because I couldn't even explain it or understand it completely. I was in healing mode. I was well enough to know it would be harmful for me to expose myself to the condemnation I was sure was attached to this list of grievances. I would be opening a door that would not let the life within me leap.

And because I was still fragile, I chose to decline the invitation.

Looking back, I see sheer desperation as the driving force behind each of my own attempts to reconcile with my church family. Why *did* I want to go back to Egypt? I can only relate it to the Battered Woman Syndrome—you want to go back to the place where the abuse is because you love who is there and you are used to it and, besides, you have nowhere else to go. Who else would want you, anyway? You're already damaged goods; you're battered and bruised and broken. Who wants to deal with someone like that?

Only Him.

Re-Buke

Throughout this period of time the abandonment issue grew excruciatingly more and more intense. I was receiving e-mail after e-mail from different people in the church who were coming up with yet another clever way to remind me I was the devil's daughter incarnate or a complete whack job. Fear would grip my heart every morning when I opened up my e-mails and received another damning message. I was being constantly reminded about what a wicked woman I was and the loudest of those voices originated in my head.

I only took the phone calls and read the e-mails because I kept waiting for one of them to be an apology. It never came and it still hasn't come. You apologize when you know you are wrong. Apparently, no one has understood that maybe, just maybe, what they have done was wrong. Or if they have, they have chosen to stay silent about it.

I understood perfectly what they were doing—they were doing what they had been trained to do. Therefore, there was nothing to apologize for. In their eyes and in their understanding, no wrong has been done. It makes sense and it became the platform to help me begin to forgive them. I knew how they were thinking because I had thought that way myself.

"Life becomes easier when you learn to accept an apology you never got." That's one of those quotes that made it on my Facebook wall. Now it would have to be my mantra.

Life, though, did not get easier. It got a whole lot sadder.

Lord, help me place my longing for apologies in Your hands.

That is one of the most difficult routes to travel: having to endure a wrong done to you and knowing, full well, that a bitter reaction to such an injustice is equally as wrong. It doesn't seem fair. It isn't fair. It wasn't fair to nail Jesus to a tree, but it happened anyway.

But in the end, it produced new life, didn't it?

Re-Store

My mind would wander to that living room window I always seemed to be peering through. Again, I was that toddler and again, no one was coming back for me. Every day I would kneel on my grandmother's couch and look out the window and wait for the car to pull into the driveway, for someone I love to get out of the car and come leaping onto the front porch and wink at me through the window shouting, "Here I am, Honey. I'm here, I'm back. I will never leave you. I will never forsake you." But it didn't happen for a long, long time.

"I was only gone four months," my Mom told me years later. Four months, a lifetime for a two-year-old. Daddy didn't come back for two years.

"Mommy! Daddy! Where are you?"

No child should have to know sorrow and fear on that level. No adult should have to carry that same wounding into the rest of their life, only to have it happen again.

This time, though, no one came back.

I know now there is a God who also saw that child and did all He could to bring her to Himself and to heal her wounds.

The church erred by addressing frailty, fault, and failure while Jesus, on the other hand, affirmed worth and value. The letter of the law can truly kill but the Spirit gives life. I was, in a sense, battling for my life. It was a war between law vs. grace and they decided to duke it out in the center of my mind.

That's where the battlefield always lies, doesn't it?

I must have chosen life because I'm here, telling you my story, knowing it might be your own, that you've heard this storyline before.

Sad.

Awkward Re-Pentance

Before the bus crash, I did once experience the joy of receiving and accepting an apology. Awkward though it might have been, it still brought healing.

In his book, *The Wild Love of God,** my youngest brother tells a compelling and beautiful story about how he was able to forgive our dad for the beatings he endured. In truth, I had no idea both my brothers were enduring the same physical abuse until the last few years. I thought, honestly, that his rage, for some strange reason, was all about me.

But I had my moment, too, after someone told me my father was a bruised reed. I had only been able to see him, up to that point, as a bruiser. It's a wonderful experience when you are able to get your thinking on the other side of the equation. It actually starts the healing process.

My moment was met in awkwardness, like my brother's was. I was well into my forties when it happened and Dad had a bit

too much to drink. His defenses came down and whatever it was that triggered it, I have no recollection. So let's just call it the Holy Spirit and not the other one.

Dad started getting nostalgic, and then apologetic, and finally he was a mass of snot and tears. He just held me in his arms while he was sitting down, and I was bent across his lap. I remember putting my hand firmly on the chair arm because I thought I was going to fall on the floor. If it was a movie script, they would have had to change our positions; it was as awkward as the repentance, but it was just as real. Reality is not balanced and doesn't photograph well.

He told me how sorry he was for hurting me all those years, and he especially was sorry about what happened that day he kept kicking me while I lay on the ground screaming.

It was easy to forgive sincerity, especially when you've waited decades for it.

My other brother never got the one-on-one, which might explain more than I would dare try to analyze on paper.

Even when they've died, it's not too late to get the broken thing fixed, is it Father-God?

Re-Demption And The Numbers Show

My brothers and I each in our own way over the years had been trying to nudge our dad toward being open to our Savior's redemption message. One day, out of the blue, Dad told my youngest brother something very strange.

"My wife and I prayed that prayer with that guy at the end of that 007 show."

"I didn't know that James Bond had a show with a prayer at the end," responded my bewildered brother.

"Well, it's the show you told me I should watch."

"Do you mean the 700 Club?"

"Yeah, whatever. They just said I'm supposed to tell somebody so I'm telling you."

And that, in a nutshell, is how my dad and his wife made their entrance into the Kingdom. Turns out it was near the end of his earthly life. He died in 1991. Our mother passed away about a year later.

My brother went on to write his book, *The Wild Love of God,** about our dad. In it he also tells of the sweet, *re-assuring* conversations he had with our dad before he died. I can see more clearly now why that title fits his story so well. This God of ours works out-of-the-box *wild* wonders all the time.

* *The Wild Love of God, A Journey into Love that Heals Life's Deepest Wounds* by Chris DuPre', copyright 2011, chrisdupre.com/products.

Let The Dead Bury The Dead

My stepmom had died and I dreaded the wake. It had nothing whatsoever to do with my stepmom and her death. She had been suffering a long time, lived a full life, had five wonderful children and loved my Dad like crazy. She also loved Jesus. I wasn't at all concerned about her: She and Dad had found the Lord, and I knew they were together again.

I was concerned about facing my brother and his wife at the wake. Yes, I'm talking about the brother who wanted to reconcile by first giving me a list of all his grievances against me. I had no idea how to behave/react/respond. I couldn't find anything in the Christian manuals on how to embrace people who no longer talk to you because you've been excommunicated and disfellowshipped from their church and their family.

I was a wreck.

Once I got to the funeral home, I knew there was no turning back. I waited outside in the hall, had a mini-meltdown at the entrance to the room and decided to go straight for the step brothers and sisters. At least, I wasn't on their hit list. And they were the ones who were really hurting. As I walked into the room, before I could reach my step siblings, my brother's wife walked over to me and gave me a hug. I stood erect and stiff, much like an ironing board, and looked at her with shock. I was not expecting to be approached and I had no words.

"I'm sorry," I stammered, "I just don't know how to respond to you."

Looking back, I don't believe there was anything else I could say. It was raw honesty. This woman, who lived half a block from my house and was married to my brother, had not spoken to me since the bus crash. I missed her terribly and now she was just inches from me, her face growing angry and red before my eyes. I actually saw her teeth come together as she gritted them in response to what I said.

"It's not about you, Carol," she replied sternly. "Your stepmother is dead."

At that point, I was not concerned with the dead. It was the living that needed my attention.

Birth Pangs

I was desperate. I seemed to be desperate a lot. Mostly I was desperate to find release from the pain of being abandoned. I'm not sure I can find the right words to describe just how deeply abandonment cuts. What is deeper than deep? What is blacker than black? What is deader than dead?

At the beginning of this pain-filled walk, I did some very stupid things that could look—dare I say it?—*crazy*. But I did them anyway. I did them because I was still learning. I did them because I was still hurting. I did them because I longed for deliverance from the pain I was carrying in my heart. It was as if I was dilated eight centimeters with no anesthesia, and no baby coming forth. I was also screaming. I scream, I've been told, at a deafening pitch.

I wanted to push this thing out before it killed me.

I knew enough about the Word and the Lord to know there is power in forgiveness. Yes, that's it. All the pain will go away if I get the forgiveness issue dealt with. So I spent one entire day making a list of everybody who ever hurt me following the bus crash. That was an intense day.

The next day, I called up each one of them on the phone and told them I forgave them for hurting me. If they weren't home, I left a message.

Intense day #2.

Stupid act #1,

Yeah, like *that* works.

Someone, please tell me what to do to make the pain go away!

So someone told me I needed to put on the whole armor of God every morning before I left the house. I play-acted the process, felt like an idiot, but did it anyway, day after day. I confessed the words in Ephesians 6 aloud as I donned myself from head to toe, in hopes I would do it "enough" times to reach that "enough" number so all the shackles would fall off and all the pain would go away.

I was dilated nine centimeters, screeching my head off by now, but still making no progress.

It was at this point I seriously considered making a pact with the devil. When you hurt so much that you think like that, you will do most anything you can to be free, rational or not. You come to a place beyond compromise. You tell the Lord He is not worth the cost of the battle or the wounds that come with it. You are ready to give up everything you believe in. No, you are ready to give up Who you believe in.

How do you begin the process of denying the One who has taken residence in your heart for decades? What brings you to the place where pain and denial meet and denial looks far more inviting?

It was not a good place to stay. Out of nowhere, at least not from anywhere inside my suffering self, came a white flag. I could only give up the fight and surrender. I still don't know how that happened except that I know now that's what God does. He rescues. He hears our cries.

I guess you could say I reached a full ten centimeters at this point and someone told me it was okay now for me to push.

Looking back, I admit to looking crazy. PTSD does that to you. I will never again doubt the workings of the mind to malfunction in response to human tragedy.

But here is where I failed. I failed to realize all those old religious tactics I used trying to set myself free were not the answer. I failed to understand I was experiencing grief at its deepest level and it was moving swiftly into the inordinate category. I failed to grasp the truth that my healing had already been shifted from the foot of the Cross to the depths of my heart.

So while I thought I was experiencing my own personal exorcism in the form of intense labor, I was actually in the process of being created into His image. My own and only involvement was to allow Him to enfold my new self under His wings. It became the purest kind of transformation mingled with the most agonizing of pain.

I failed to understand I was not the one who was in labor.

I was the one who was being birthed.

April Showers

It was just another ordinary day in the desert: dry, rough, hot, lonely. I asked the Lord if He loved me and got the same response the last time I asked Him that question, which left **me** dry, rough, hot and lonely.

Silence.

It didn't help that it was April. April in my state is like November, though somewhat forgiving because the months that follow eventually bring summer, and summer at best is less than the full and official three months long. Within and without, I lived in a dark place.

It was late afternoon when I pushed myself out the door to get the mail. My eye caught something red that appeared to be floating on my front lawn. My lawn was at its ugly stage—soggy and brown and void of life.

That was like my heart, as well, except not the soggy part. My heart was parched.

The object that caught my eye was a balloon, still filled with some degree of helium, making it dance around the front yard with the gentle breeze. It was shaped like a heart. White letters spelled out the words I LOVE YOU in its center.

It made no difference that it might have been a leftover from February. It arrived, I can only believe, at my house, at this time, on this very grey day, by divine design.

As I walked back into the house, embracing the balloon, water trickled into my hardened soil and tiny buds exploded under my feet.

Transplant

"Lord, my life is shit!"

I was shocked at my own words. I was addressing God. I was standing at my front door, and it was opened, and the neighborhood encircled me because I lived in the middle house on a cul-de-sac so I was always surrounded by something.

I call Him Lord or Daddy or Father when I talk. Sometimes Papa, since I read *The Shack*.* But we do talk. And it was my voice that was the loudest that day.

Most days, it is, anyway. He's a whisperer. We humans all have little voices, if you were to compare them to, say, thunder claps, so I raise mine just a bit and believe that my every word is heard through all the other sounds in the universe. Like in the movie, *God Almighty*. He pulls out my words amid the clang of other sounds and other voices. He hears only *my* voice and listens intently. What I have to say is *that* important to Him and since I was relearning us as a couple, I was not sure how best to approach Him.

I was trying to tell Him what my true feelings were about the direction my life had taken and it took a lot for me to use that word. Maybe it's normal vocabulary for someone else's mouth, but it just didn't normally have place in mine.

But then things have changed. I've changed. This day, it was a perfect word to use and it spoke with clarity and it spoke with boldness and it spoke well of my life.

I shut up long enough to let Him talk and He gave me a new perspective on life.

"Have you ever thought seriously about what you call 'shit' before today? Or about what the grossest thing to come out of ANY body is used for?"

Not really.

"It's used for fertilizer, honey. It helps things to grow faster and better. It is sweetness coming out of stench; it is renewal coming out of repulsion. It is life coming out of death.

"I'm going to take your life and plant it in another garden and you will see it grow. First the natural and then the spiritual."

The following week, I found a wallpaper border in a clearance bin that appeared to be a series of attractive and colorful

birdhouses, but were actually outhouses. I bought three of them and lined my office with it as a reminder.

It became a conversation piece, too.

* *The Shack,* a novel by Wm. Paul Young, self-published 2007; Windblown Media;, reissue edition, 2011.

Joy

The first two people who greatly influenced my life when I started my journey into the desert were named Joy and Grace. I'm not making this up. You would think I'd see the obvious, but when you're focusing so deeply on your navel, as I most certainly was, these kinds of things go right over your head.

You've heard about Grace.

Joy actually entered first.

Our paths reconnected in a place that welcomed dialogue. The nightmare I was going through easily made its way into the conversation, as I made sure it always did. I told everybody about everything and I told them too much about each thing. Joy knew instantly what I needed and she went home, went on-line and ordered a book for me to read.

Let me say something here. When people become aware that you're hurting or suffering through a painful time or experiencing personal tragedy, they like to give you a book that, at one point in *their* healing process, helped them. They assume it will help *you.* People did that for me and it was a kindly gesture from all of them. My bookshelves are stocked full of good intentions. Some I have devoured, some I have only glimpsed through, and some I knew instantly would only become fillers for a barren bookshelf. The ones I hated the most left me wondering if I might have missed out on the original born-again experience. They went into the circular file.

But not one of the books I was given was as useful as the one Joy bought for me. It became my first "devoured" book. I consumed it right away.

I also wept deeply at the revelation it brought.

I have never lent that particular book out to anyone. I wrote comments all over the margins and underlined specific examples and used the word WOW a lot, including an enlarged size of the WOW, depending on how deeply I was touched. The book is chock full of exclamation marks, with references in the margins to specific names and experiences in my own history. I read about situations and circumstances that defined, to a T, what I had been through. The fact that they were written by somebody who never met me, someone who never knew my story, blew me away.

What I thought was my story, I soon learned, had happened to other people in other places. This book became my *never-doubt-that-you've-heard-from-God* proof, my *you're-not-the-only-one* evidence, my *others-understand-because-they've-been-there* testimonial.

The book is all about spiritual abuse. It is *The Subtle Power of Spiritual Abuse, Recognizing and Escaping Spiritual Manipulation and False Spiritual Authority Within the Church*, written by David Johnson and Jeff VanVonderen, a pastor and a Christian psychologist.

I bought a second, unmarked copy for loaning purposes only. I wanted to get the word out, to give other hurting people a book that helped me. I assumed it would help them.

I pray it will never become a filler for a barren bookshelf or find its way to the circular file.

Joy Again

Joy did something else for me, something she would be shy about revealing but I am not shy, so I'm going to tell on her.

For one full year, she took me to a Christian counselor once a week and paid for my sessions each time. This gave me opportunity to learn four things:

1) I was not crazy.

2) I was exhibiting symptoms of PTSD.

3) Other people in the area were aware of how unhealthy things were in my church as far as leadership control was concerned.

4) There aren't a lot of people in this world as kind as Joy.

New And Used

It is amazing to me how the brain gets short-circuited following a trauma.

All I wanted was a bathrobe like the one I was wearing now—the one I wore every night—the one made out of chenille that wrapped around, tied at the waist, fell 54" to my ankles, had a hooded collar, and was size M. No buttons, no zippers. (Too

260

hard to hook and buckle before the first cup of coffee). I wasn't too concerned about color because I'd put enough stipulations on it already. Besides, bathrobes are meant to be felt on the inside. The outsides are for others to see. I didn't much care what others saw, now that I lived alone. Few saw me this way, anyway.

The robe I had now, the old one, came with an apology, whenever I got caught wearing it. "It's chenille," I told the few people who did catch me in it. "It's supposed to do that." *That* was pill. It was supposed to lose its tufted lines and as it did, it made flat, barren spaces on a canvas of soft pinky-peach. It was bag lady appropriate but I didn't much care. It was warm and the hood made it warmer and I lived alone in cold, northern weather where winters start on Halloween and end, if you're lucky, the day after Easter. I would put the hood up to keep warm. I also used it for devotions because I thought God wouldn't speak to me unless my head was covered, but that's for another time and another chapter altogether.

My insistence on the chenille fabric brought back memories of my grandmother. I always pictured her in the morning, wearing a chenille robe and wrapping it around my cold little body like grandmothers do. I now better understood my drive to get one like it. I searched the local stores over a period of three years and finally concluded that chenille bathrobes were not the rage at this time. Someone I don't know who lives in a warmer climate and makes a ton of money decided that for me. I tried the internet, dared to walk the streets of E-Bay and learned that chenille is for nursing home residents and maybe I could find myself a used one. That would be like wearing someone's underpants and I scratched myself at the thought of it.

261

I checked the label of my old robe and typed the brand name into Google. In just seconds I crossed the ocean and found myself in a rich and colorful exchange of words with an Irishman who checked the stock, the back room, and the rejects, and could not find me what I wanted. He named a little boutique in Brooklyn, a scant 7-hour drive from my home, that sold the brand I was looking for, and so I called them. A Jewish woman who answered the phone regretted they *had only one robe left, so sorry*. It was a size medium, 54" long, tied at the waist, had a hood and was a rich sapphire blue in color.

It was also four times what I would have spent on a bathrobe. *Yes, we can mail it for an extra $11.00* and within three business days, I was wearing a robe of sapphire royalty, convincing myself daily that it was worth the price to get this kind of perfection, this kind of warmth, this kind of nostalgia.

The following week, with no preparation, no internet search and a limited budget, I went to a used car dealership and bought the first car I test drove. My only stipulation was the color.

My mind was healing, but slowly, very slowly.

Chapter Fourteen

Grad School

Two Schools Of Thought

During this time of what?...growth?...transition?, it was painfully obvious the charismatic church system in my area wanted nothing to do with me. So I tried hiding myself away in the confines of the educational system. I'd always loved college, never had a real job, had no skills outside of helping to pastor the flock, so I decided I needed to leave the area for a while and obtain knowledge.

Of course, the first place I attended was a Bible school. Of course. I was convinced it held the answers and a possible future for me. It was all about Jesus, after all, and maybe somebody there would understand what I just came out of and be somewhat sympathetic to my needs.

It didn't take long to discover it only held more of what seemed like legalism to me.

I had to go out and buy a ton of dresses because we weren't allowed to wear pants. Of course, they had to cover my knees. I personally preferred that length, but it had nothing to do with modesty and everything to do with covering up my varicose veins.

Because the school deals with mostly young people, there were curfews and demerits and I had to get special permission to be exempt from working around the campus or going on field trips to witness at the mall.

I was washing my hands in the bathroom near the chapel one day when one of the young students was complaining about

all the rules and restrictions. I said to her, "You know, I wonder if the reason they have all that is to see what kind of attitudes will come out of the students about it. They might just want to find out if there is rebellion hidden in the heart."

At this point, we heard a stir in one of the stalls. You never know who might be listening in on your conversation. Sure enough, one of the older professors who had been there a long time emerged and said, "That is exactly why we do it."

So this time I saw the legalism for what it was and found it easy to follow the rules because I'd already been doing that so well for so long. Still, when I left after a year of studies, I had only made two friends, encountered that rental case man,* and had a little more bondage to work through.

My second school was at the local university, in the Creative Writing Master's Program. It was in this atmosphere that I went to the other extreme in an effort to discover who I was, minus the legalities. I called what I went through on that campus "post-menopausal puberty." It became an educational experience on a variety of levels. I was free to swear and say terrible things and even show off my varicose veins with the clam diggers I wore. The swearing didn't work for me, the Holy Spirit did a lot of purging in regards to my attitude, but I did like the clam diggers and even now have a lot of them in my closet.

By the time I had worked my way through these two college experiences, I probably learned more about who I was not, than who I actually was.

I was in my mid-60's and having an identity crisis.

I had had an identity crisis *in* the mid-1960's and thought we were done with this.

I learned as long as Jesus is Lord and we're still breathing, we're not done with school.

*Chapter 9, "Rental Case," page 190

Waterproof

"*Go to the water,*" my Christian Insurance Agent told me.

I thought I was being directed to a new church. "The Water" had a genuine ring to it.

We had been having a little discussion over the phone about the high cost of car insurance for an old lady who averaged 6,000 miles a year on her ten-year-old car and how wonderful Jesus was. I told him I couldn't find a church that welcomed me, besides the little quiet congregation. I told him I wanted to go back to college and get my Master's Degree in Creative Writing. I told him I had gotten accepted into the program but didn't have the money to go. I told him I was turned down for both the Fellowship and the Assistantship I had applied for.

I told him too much.

We never even met, not even to this day, but there were very few Christians who would talk to me and so we talked. And he told me to go to the water.

It turned out to be a word of wisdom for me. I headed to the local body of water, a canal. It was a warm July day and the sun was actually shining. So I just sat there on a bench not meant for most healthy posteriors and waited for the clouds to part or a dolphin to leap out of the murky waters.

Nothing happened. And I gave God a full hour of meditation, too. On the way back to my car, the Lord spoke to me and told me I would be given the provision to go to graduate school.

When I got home, there was a message on my phone machine to call the graduate office, that they had good news for me. The woman who won the Fellowship I wanted had turned it down. I was number two on the list. Did I want it?

I had first met the Lord in 1973, in the last two weeks of my undergraduate studies. I had been accepted to an Ivy League graduate school for my Master's Degree. When I met the Lord, I knew I was to stay put where I was, and turned down the scholastic opportunity of a lifetime.

"Thank you for giving this to me back then," I heard the Lord say. *"This is payback."*

School was also a whole lot harder. I was in my twenties back then. The Fellowship was called The Diversity Fellowship and I had met the diversity criteria for that year: I was old.

Ivy Covered Outhouse

My old church often referred to the local college as a hell hole. Having attended it as a full-time student, who was also a senior citizen, I would probably have to call it a toilet bowl. This description, however, has nothing to do with what I found happening on the campus; it more clearly defined what I used it for. As a creative writing major in the Master's program, I used it as an outlet for my present state of mind. That state included anger, frustration, turmoil, wounding, retaliation and retribution. I wrote stories about death, murder, mental illness, revenge, and debauchery.

Both I and my writings were fully accepted on that campus because the people there, professors and students alike, were not sin-conscious. There is a good side to being like that. You are simply accepted on the mere fact that you exist. It helps, too, to have a brain and a talent. I knew I had both, but the acceptance thing was something I had lost with the bus crash. I sucked it in. I was desperate for the attention.

It is no wonder that I wandered around that campus in confusion, especially that first semester. It is no wonder that I upchucked the last four years of my life onto thousands of pieces of paper and called it stories and completed assignments. One teacher pushed me to get even "creepier" with my little ditties, so I pushed it past comfortable for me and took some of my stories into the same pit I had just climbed out of. Of course I got an A, but deep down inside, I felt like I didn't make the grade with the Lord.

"Get it out, honey," I heard the Lord say.

It turned out to be a real case of purging for me, an exorcism of sorts that allowed me to empty myself of the anger and the hurt and the frustration that was ripping me apart on the inside. It was what I thought it was—a safe place. He said He would take care of any cleaning up that was needed, in me, on the campus, even in my thesis.

"What you say right now is really just a whole lot of flesh and frustration pouring out. Let it purge you. Let Me clean you out. The world will give you a Master's Degree in English and I will get you a Decree by the Master to write the story behind the story."

Which is why you are reading this. Which is why I know that this paragraph is full of incomplete sentences. Which is why I don't care because it's not as important as knowing that God is good and what He does is good.

It's just that it's easier to see His goodness after the junk gets flushed out first.

Class Clown

It was my favorite class—sitting around the large, rectangular table and getting critiqued on the written homework assignment. We never had to worry that any comments would sting. We knew they would. The professor—one of my personal favorite personalities—made sure we'd get lambasted if he didn't like what we wrote. He had a knack for searching out the tiniest mistake and supersizing it until all your ego flew out the room's one tiny window.

He would make a great Sadducee.

What he did push was a gross-me-out button. He preferred we write about the dark side and then go even darker. I played easily to his instructions.

There was a new girl in the group this year, a tiny little thing and pretty as can be, a newlywed, she told us. She was a dance major but wanted to touch lightly on writing—her other interest. She had no idea we did not touch lightly in this class. She never told us her full name, just her first name and the last name initial. It worked.

Once again, I used this opportunity to explode on paper, remembering that twenty-something, unregenerate brain cells didn't care what the old lady was writing.

My college mantra came from Aristotle: "It is the mark of an educated mind to be able to entertain a thought without accepting it." I entertained a lot and accepted so little.

About a third of the way through the semester, she told a story about herself that included stating the first name of her husband and the location of the house he grew up in. She was married to someone from the church I had just been excommunicated from and chances were, she'd heard the history of her new fellowship and my name might have come up a time or twenty.

By then, it was too late to apologize, if I cared to, and too late to explain, if I could. I got an A but may have lost a few grade points in the Kingdom.

But He said He would take care of the messes. So I have to assume He has.

Semester Break

When it came time for me to write my thesis, I compiled all my writings from the last two years and invented a way to creatively categorize them. I was to be, after all, a *creative* writing major. The majority of my stories expressed the frustrations of growing old with the added dimension of boxing my way out of the insanity that had been my life. I titled it AGED WHINE and while I was still not thinking in a straight line, that's probably the very thing that made me a good student and a better writer.

But the Jesus part of me didn't know where to fit in. I loved Him, thought about Him all the time, stuck religiously to my daily devotions and church hopped more than your average bunny rabbit.

When I read some of those stories, today, I cringe. Did I really say that? Are those thesis papers really in a bound book and do they sit in that back office on a shelf allowing free access to anyone who wants to read them? Will I kick myself in the proverbial backside for saying what I said?

I have a brother who sings and composes and when anyone mentions his first CD, he is embarrassed by it. It was, after all, just the beginning of something that is now so improved in quality, performance, and spiritual growth that it seems both shameful and embarrassing to mention it might even exist.

My first drawing wasn't much to look at or my early days of potty training anything worth taking the time to ponder. Growth steps, shame, and embarrassment often come in the same package.

I don't know about you, but I have a lot of things I did in those early years of wandering around in the desert that make me blush with the thought. Yet, with the hindsight I've been given, I delight at the growth and the change. It is called life and learning and if it serves to be a stepping stone to a higher place in the Kingdom, then such is life.

Separation

I pounded on the mattress with my fist and jumped out of bed screaming "Get out of my life," at the top of my lungs. I told you outright, "I have had it with you and I no longer want us to be together. Life with you is too hard and you are absent far more than you are present and that is <u>not</u> the way a couple is supposed to be." I slept on the couch and watched TV until I finally fell asleep. In the morning, I virtually ignored you as you tried to woo me back.

There comes a time when you have to take a stand and speak up. There comes a time when you are not walking in agreement and someone needs to walk away. There comes a time when the pressure is so great and the affection is so shallow and the commitment is so shaky that separation is the only way to sanity.

I separated. I sought sanity.

I emptied myself in mindless computer games and hollow television shows and once, on a very bad day, a second glass of wine. I was forced to let you stay, but only on another level of the house, refusing to respond to your advances.

You made promises I was sure you would never keep. You spoke affectionately and I turned away, not believing your words. I carried your love letters to a far-away storage area but feared destroying them, admitting in my heart that an ounce of hope still remained and that it was possible we would be able to work through the relationship, that you and I would find a common ground, a place we could both agree on and work from. I rationalized the possibility. I waited for you to see what it was that I was now seeing, and that you would admit your failure to be the husband you had promised me you would be so many years ago.

But you would not budge, insisting you were the one who was right and in this case, once again, I was wrong. My heart grew cold again as I waited for you to respond, to change, to see my point of view, but you refused, arguing that it was my need to change that needed to be addressed. You refused to compromise in any way.

We lived like this far too long and fooled, as it says, "even the elect."

I left you waiting a long time before I opened my heart and began to understand what was really going on between us, realizing this is something I needed to face and not walk away from; that I must allow myself to be overwhelmed and overtaken with the idea that I may have it all wrong and maybe, just maybe, you might be seeing something in me that up until now, I have been unable to see in myself.

My heart grew warm toward you, and I allowed you in again.

You are, after all, God, and I am, after all, Yours.

Chapter Fifteen

Hearing From God Again

Hearing Test

Until I sold my kitchen table and chairs to pay the monthly mortgage, I sat at it every morning and gave the Lord my first fruits. They were not particularly fresh and plump at 6 AM, but I felt He understood they were enough. This particular morning, I had one question weighing especially heavily on my mind that had been plaguing me for quite a long time. "What purpose ……..?" Not expecting an answer really, I heard a voice tell me something that seemed very stupid and I naturally dismissed it. It remained persistent and got louder so I challenged its credibility. It was not my imagination. I was incapable of coming up with the statement:

"What I have for your life is halfway between your two favorite books of the Bible."

I decided to play the voice's game. I already knew what those two books were.

I have always been drawn to Genesis, especially, as laid out earlier, the story of Adam and Eve and the first sin and who does what to whom and why. Ephesians, particularly chapter four, carried a message to me about church unity that drew me in that first year I walked with the Lord; that kept me moving toward the goal during those three decades spent as a pastor's wife; and that kept the glimmer of hope from being totally snuffed out after the bus crash. This unity factor was something I had never been able to escape. I sensed its fulfillment was only just beginning.

It became a no-brainer—find out what page Ephesians was

on and divide the page number by two. I was curious. I wanted to know where the voice was really coming from.

The halfway point was in Psalms, Psalm 66 to be exact. I gasped when I opened to that page. The year before, I had circled verse 16, dated it, and made a comment in the side margin, "This is my calling."

"Come and hear, all you who fear God, and I will declare what He has done for my soul."

I asked the Lord, "Why did you do that?" and got the most simple of answers: *"Because there will be times when I will ask you to do something that will not make sense and I want you to be sure you know My voice."*

Like, start writing your first book at the same time you begin collecting Social Security and Medicare.

Dedication

It took me just over a year-and-a-half to be able to walk into my daughter's bedroom without crying. She had moved out when her Daddy and I split up and she was the last of what I thought I still had left. Her room would now have to become a source of income. I spent three full days painting, cleaning, and preparing it for what would be the beginning of many years of horrifying and off-beat renting experiences. They were unarguably some of the worst nightmares of my already nightmarish life, and if I am to give glory to God, their stories may never be written. It is not always easy to see "all things work out for good" in the middle of strange encounters, even years later.

Just looking at my daughters' abandoned possessions was a painful experience. They included, among all the other things, a Precious Moments figurine on her nightstand, the one her father and I received as a gift the day we dedicated her to the Lord. It was of a little boy and a little girl, standing on a platform. The boy held the baby and the girl held the Bible. I pushed past the melancholy and the hurt and continued the cleansing and cleaning process.

As I reached out to remove it, I saw that it was broken. The little boy had separated from the platform and I could not help but think, adding to my sadness, that this is exactly what had happened in our own home. Like the figurine, he was not standing with me and he had our daughter with him. I wondered if it had been broken by accident or with intent.

I began doing the pouting thing, as only I can do. Father saw it and spoke very clearly to me.

"So where does that leave YOU?"

I looked at the two pieces I held, one in each hand.

Still standing, I thought.

"And what is that in your hand?" He asked.

It's the Word, Your Word.

"And what is that in the back of the little boy's head?"

I turned the figurine over and saw a gaping hole where the back of his head should have been.

I smiled, for the first time in months.

Cute, Dad.

The Splotch

I live in an area that is six months winter and the remaining three seasons are squeezed into the remaining six months. That's the norm for a northern climate. Dark. Cold. Persistent. Seems like I say that a lot, and I do because it's true. Healing seems harder to achieve without natural sunlight.

I stood in the middle of my main living area—one large room with a cathedral ceiling and three sky-light windows, all encompassing the kitchen, dining area, and living-room—and decided to paint earth's sunshine on its walls. It took me an inordinately long time to mix the yellows with the golds and whites to match the ceramic tiles on the floor, to breathe life into a space that was swallowing me up in clay beige. While finding the right shade of gold took a number of days, it took just two days to do the actual painting.

After the first full day of work, I laid newspaper on the guest room floor, taking every precaution to protect the newly laid golden brown carpet   I set the paint can and assorted tools on the newspaper and went to bed. My living area seemed a tad brighter.

The next morning, I collected the paint and tools and noticed that a large glob of that paint had somehow imbedded itself under the newspaper and within the carpeting. Smack-dab in the middle of the entranceway into the room, it lay, exposed, distracting, ugly. All the scrubbing in the world didn't remove a single trace of the stain and I was heartsick. I quit trying and battled more depression as I finished the project I had started in the living area. It wasn't until later that morning that I realized the stain had moved to another location.

Days before, I had set a prism on the window ledge of that guest room, hoping for some color to be reflected on the walls when the morning sun hit it just right. When the light reflected through the prism and onto the carpet, it showed up as a splotch.

I was trying to remove a rainbow.

"You can't erase a rainbow," Jesus told me.

"I made promises to you that no one will have the power to erase, including, and most especially, you."

Lip Locking

It was something I had heard for years and readily did without question. The preacher was giving his sermon and simply said, "Repeat after me," to which the audience, myself included, repeated after him whatever it was he was saying.

When I was in the early stages of the Holy Spirit recovery program, I would hear this said from time to time by various preachers and immediately tightened my lips, squinted my eyes, and ended up making a lemon-sucking face.

No way am I gonna do what you say, mister. You can't make me.

It's a pretty common reaction to legalism. It's a guard against another takeover, imagined or real. Still, it's a decade later and it hasn't gone away.

Chances are, you don't know what you're repeating until it's said. I take no chances on confessing with my mouth unless I'm prepared ahead of time about it.

I'll repeat a Scripture verse, anytime. But don't tell me what to do when I don't know what I'm about to do.

Is that unhealthy? Who cares? It's safe and safe is what I need.

Foot Fetish

You know the footsteps story—the one set of footprints in the sand are all you see because it's Jesus who carried you through the hard times.

A few years ago, a new set of prints made its way on the internet. This time, there were two pairs of footprints, one somewhat larger in size than the other, both zigzagging their way across the computer screen. We were told the larger set belonged to Jesus and the other set of footprints were your own and the two of you were dancing.

I have a vision, too. I see a pair of footprints walking along the sands of what I can only assume is that same bit of ground— except this time, I am positive the sands are those of a desert and not a beach. Behind these ever-moving-forward footprints are two horizontal stripes, approximately eight inches apart and running the entire length of the desert floor.

"Lord, what is that?" my quivering voice asked.

"Carol, that's Me, dragging you through the last several years of your life."

The Other Tuesday Morning

My Tuesday morning group is expecting great things from me. It has nothing to do with my gifts or my talents or my calling; it has nothing to do with me. They expect great things from everybody.

I've been woven into a roomful of Godly women who meet on a Tuesday morning in a living room far too small for the number of women who show up, making fellowship ultra-cozy. Each of these women embrace the new face and the new crisis and the new girl on the block and they don't ask her what church she goes to or stick a thermometer in her mouth to gauge her spiritual temperature.

All the while, these same women never forget the ones who have been there, year after year, decade after decade, extending the same love and courtesy to them, showing the world around them what I have come to believe is the true meaning of church.

The women are a rare collection of Body parts, YOUR Body parts, Lord, used these last three decades to bandage broken bodies, pour oil into raw and flaming wounds, locate the key to the prison door, and reawaken the hearts religion nearly destroyed.

And always, always reminding each other of their worth and value.

I see Jesus when I come to these meetings and, if nothing else, this might actually be a rare peek into His feminine side.

Chapter Sixteen

Healing is all about him

Root System

When I bought the house I live in now, I noticed rust stains around the drain in the tub and commented to the owners that I would like to see that problem "cleaned up" before the closing date. The tub was immaculate when I moved in. Problem solved.

I didn't live here but one day when I realized the tub faucet dripped on a regular basis. While the tub looked immaculate, it wouldn't take long for it to look like it did the first time I saw it. Problem not solved.

I don't think it's any different from the way we deal with so many of our own personal stains. It's the old cliché about putting a Band-Aid on a cancer and calling it healed. It's going to show up, sooner or later, and it might not be so easy to fix, or maybe too late to fix. A good God goes directly into the root system and pulls out the problem's source. It hurts like hell, too. It IS hell. It is hell coming out, and that's a good thing.

I just recently hired a plumber to fix the tub.

Jesus will just have to fix the other parts that make up me, the parts that still leak and leave stains.

There are days when I prefer the Band-Aid treatment; but while He can be gentle, He must, I have to admit, always be thorough.

Wading

I stick my head in another toilet bowl and clean out the brown stains, reminding myself I might have to do this for a while and if I would just plough through and not think so hard about what I was doing, it might not be all that bad. A strange combination of humiliation and humility merge together in my head—or is it my heart—while I try to figure out why my life had come to this. Again.

I now, professionally, clean up other people's *grossities*. *Microsoft Word* doesn't recognize the word *grossities*, but I clearly do. I'm cleaning it.

I used to do it for nothing. I used to do it because I wanted to do it, because my heart was grateful to be resurrected from the dead and I wasn't sure how to thank the Lord, so I began cleaning the church annex on a regular basis. The annex was a house attached to my new church, a type of rectory where a lot of teens and twenty-something's congregated when the massive wave of the Jesus movement fell on us in the early 70's. I remember the youth pastor sticking his head in the bathroom door while I had my head in the toilet bowl and commenting that God must have some wonderful things planned for my life because I was "manifesting servant hood."

I had no idea what he was talking about. I just felt so grateful myself, to be clean and whole again. And besides, the toilets in that place *were* pretty gross and I didn't see anyone else offering to do it.

Now, nearly forty years later and a recent Medicare recipient, I am doing the same thing for all the wrong reasons. I need to make some money because I don't have enough to live on. I sense I am not grateful for this opportunity and might be manifesting something far more sinister and certainly not servant hood.

Today, that same youth pastor no longer speaks to me. But if he did, he might tell me, like my daughter has done, that I deserve this, that I am reaping all I have sown and all of this is just full-circle stuff coming at me. And yet the Lord, in His sovereignty, in His goodness and in His mercy, speaks to me in the midst of these *grossities*, and reminds me of His plan for my life, that it is wonderful indeed and the latter will far exceed the former.

I just hope He's referring to my life and not toilet bowls.

Wedded Blitz

"Our marriage was made in heaven."

I remember, as a baby Christian, being told that by a member of my newly-found church.

I would watch his relationship with his wife so I might glean what made it so filled with bliss. It took very little time to see exactly whose heaven this was; it was heaven for his wife. She was in complete control of everything and her husband used the phrase, *"Yes, dear,"* on a regular basis.

It was this very type of woman my husband was afraid I would become. I was far more outspoken and louder than most

women he knew. But I wanted so much to do the right thing by standing in the right place in relation to him.

I realized early on it was off to one side and just slightly to the rear.

We were considered an odd couple, one of God's unusual but holy mixes—odd because I was loud and boisterous and he was mostly steady and calm. Of one thing I was absolutely sure: this man was the right choice for me and I was as sure of that as I was about my own salvation.

The way our marriage went was typical of most married couples, I'd say. We had wonderful times and challenging times, exasperating times and memorable times. We grew, we struggled, we did everything we could to keep the relationship going and working. As things got shaky, we sought counsel. We studied the wisdom made available in Christian books and manuals.

I don't know about him, but after all the counseling in offices and books, I began to wonder if I was sitting on a Petri dish and being used as an experiment. I felt "worked over" most of the time. I suppose that was how I should have felt, because the majority of the counsel pointed to me who was at fault and me who had to change and me who should be completely submitted to whatever my husband said and did, whether he was right or wrong. So many times my husband would tell me what I believed or felt or thought or did was simply not normal. After a while, and to please both him and the Lord, I had no other recourse but to believe what I was told.

It was far heavier a load than I was able to carry but I can say I honestly tried to carry it right up until the time I developed a sort of spiritual hernia and needed repair. I had no idea how to take this to the Cross and yet the Cross was the only place built for burdens like this. That's just about the time the lady came into my kitchen and helped me unload what was weighing me down.

I learned years later, and with hindsight, all those things my husband told me were not normal in our marriage were simply common to all of mankind. I can see now that there was some kind of invisible bar he had set for me that was placed not only out of my line of vision but out of the range of possibility.

Someone once said that if you stop loving a person it means you never loved them before, because true love doesn't stop loving. I'm not sure where to go with that, but I am fully certain I still love that man. Even with all the terrible things he did and said prior to our break-up, I see him in the light of all I've learned over the years since, and my heart aches for his loss that comes with his misunderstanding of Christianity and submission and women. And himself in Christ.

I recently told a friend of his that I felt sorry for him and hoped he'd have an epiphany about what really happened. The friend laughed and said, *"He said the exact same thing about you."*

And as nice as it would be for us to be on the same page, we are, in reality, in the same book—the Book of Life. He is no longer my husband, but he is most certainly my brother.

I was reminded, in those early stages following the bus crash that the same grace being poured out to me was also being poured out on my persecutors. That included my daughter, my pastor, my one brother, my church family, and even my husband. I knew this was a love I did not yet comprehend.

Slow Down—Road Work Ahead

I admit to still learning who Carol DuPre' really is outside of marriage and outside of the interpretations of others. All my life I can attest to being just a hair off of the road everyone else seemed to be traveling. I didn't fit into a religious mode at all. My resistance was misinterpreted as rebellion. I was told I was odd, unusual, different, strange, and weird. "Unique" was brought up and I chose it as the best description because it didn't connote off-the-wall. I have since learned that this uniqueness is a gift and it is who I am. I hear the Lord a lot telling me there are things in me that others don't like that actually ARE me, that they don't need changing or apology, and I have to (my thoughts here) get thicker skin. So many people in the Body of Christ (myself included) are trying to change and rearrange a pre-determined personality into what they think someone should be. If I'm a belly-button, don't tell me how to flex my muscles if I don't have any!

I wish I wasn't still a work in progress. I wish I'd already arrived. I suppose that means I wish I had already reached a state of perfection and the Lord would take me home or let me off the hook. He wouldn't press me for more time with Him, He'd back out of the way when it came to decision-making because for sure I'd make the right choice and those times of desperation and fear would be replaced with confidence and strength. That feeling I get when I know I've screwed up, deep in the bowels of my belly—I'd never feel it again.

That won't happen. He loves me too much, as they say, to let me stay this way: beautifully flawed within the confines of my own physical self. He sees me perfected and I see Him perfecting. It's a sure sign that we love each other.

Fill In The Blank

'Tell me what this giving thing is all about," I inquired of the Lord.

I was struggling with everything I'd ever been told for the last thirty years. I didn't even trust the basics. I told the Lord, "I don't get this giving thing anymore but I don't want to be a hoarder either."

Such a dumb thing to say. I didn't have enough extra money to put aside that would bring me even remotely close to a state of hoarder-ship. But I knew in my heart that money shouldn't possess my heart, so I asked Him to show me what to do with mine.

Immediately He put a number in my head—$350.00. Make out a check, sign and date it, and leave the *Pay to the Order of* blank. I walked around with that blank check for days, anticipating His voice for the choice, when I ran into someone I knew to be happy most of the time and saw that she wasn't. She was a heavy set woman, about my age, with short, black hair that was always much too dark for her complexion or her age. She was crying.

"For the first time in my life, I had to go on welfare," she told me. I knew she was what people might call *slow;* I would call it *gravely injured.* Life had dealt her a series of hardships and the *slow* was more like heavily medicated on prescription drugs—the kind that numbs the inner pain while glazing the outer face. She was a hard worker, she always had a job, even if it was simple or tedious. Waiting for the federal monies to come in left her with a small space of time where no money was coming in at all and now she had crossed paths with me during the "no-money" phase.

I had something. It was a blank check waiting for a name. It was a no-brainer.

I filled in the blank line with her name, folded the check and told her it was from the Lord and that He loved her. She thanked me, hugged me and left the store we were in.

She was back in less than thirty seconds.

"Last night I got down on my knees," she shouted, "And I told the Lord I needed $350.00 to get by until my first check came in." We hugged and cried for a really long time; two sisters in Christ, two distinctly different prayers answered by one listening, caring, educating Father.

Names

Sometimes the only sign of spring you get where I live is roadkill. I've seen it all—woodchucks, squirrels, deer and mostly the not-so-swift raccoon. Ugly. It's always ugly. Uglier still is when I see a dead animal on the road that probably has a name. It's a dog or a cat and I can't look at it and not feel a pain in my heart as I drive by.

Somebody's going to cry themselves to sleep tonight.

I've done that a few times myself.

Real roadkill doesn't have a name. Pets have a name. You love them so much you give them a name and when they learn it, they respond to you. Farmers tell their children never to name the animals they raise for food or the big dinner is pretty much ruined.

Sometimes when a woman endures the heartache of a miscarriage, the child is often given a name and sometimes, too, a funeral service. There's an endearing thing going on here, a love connection. You care deeply and you give something or someone a name.

The Lord knows us by name, as well. Mine, I'm told, is written in a very important book and it's specially chosen for me. It means *song of joy* and I'm on the verge of entering into that definition fully as we walk out these remaining years together. I am, at the very least, privileged to know Him back and honored to know His name. I call Him all kinds of endearing names that reflect all kinds of endearing titles. He earned every one of them.

Savior, Lord, Father, Papa. Names above all other names.

Father

I would like to welcome the Trinity back into my life.

Father. Son. Holy Spirit.

The whole oneness concept got so out of hand that we actually changed the words around in one of the most beloved hymns on the planet.

"God in three persons, blessed trinity" became "God in Christ Jesus, blessed unity." *

Yes, indeed, we were the cutting edge.

After the bus crash, and long into my healing, I suddenly found You guys making Your way into my spirit and my thought patterns. Once again, You seemed to come out of nowhere and suddenly, there You were. And You began to reveal Yourselves to me and it helped me to know You and love You afresh.

Father. I cannot be afraid of Your name. I cannot be afraid of Your title. We've put it in front of the priests' last names and more likely than not, they have never had that reproductive experience. We've ripped the Father heading to shreds or dropped it altogether and called it misogynistic, prejudice, controlling, domineering. We remember our own fathers and all their flaws and many of us find the connection horrific instead of holy.

You will never find a love like parent to child. The intensity is beyond anything we can even find words for, so we stop using words and rely on embraces and kisses and crying and song. Watch a videotaped childbirth and tell me you were not touched in some way by the presence of what can only be described as sheer joy.

Father. You were always the original seed planter.

I need someone to watch me and watch what I do; someone to listen to my every word and yes, even my every thought. I need someone to tell me how pleased He is to know me and to give me a high-five when I get something right. And I need Him to tell me to face things head-on when I would rather turn my back or when I say to Him "Talk to the hand." I need Him to remind me He will be with me and we'll face it together.

I could try this life on my own, but my compass would never point north and I would never find where my true home exists.

We were made for this. We were birthed for this.

For Father.

* From the hymn, "Holy, Holy, Holy."

Son

I have never had a son and my only child, a daughter, was adopted. I cannot identify with knowing what it is like to bear or raise a son but I can say, with confidence, that the adoption process was just as painful, just as joy-filled, and just as intense as the rest of you fruitful people comprehended about your own.

But the Son. The Son of God. And you shall call His name Jesus. I called His name. I called Jesus! Jesus! Jesus! You have to help me. You have to save me. You have to rescue me. You have to take my sin away. You have to be the father I misunderstood, the husband who left me, the brother I lost in the bus crash.

I think Jesus is the one I talk to the most. While He may have put the face on God, He also did all the legwork and He knows the routine and I think I identify more with the someone who's been there/done that/worn the...

Worn the stripes. Worn the crown. Worn the shame.

I never forget that we're related. I never forget that He's committed to our relationship. I never forget that He totally gets me.

He is my substitute. He took to the Cross what I am ashamed to even admit I have ever embraced. He has become my father and my husband and my brother and He can handle all the drama that comes with each position.

He makes our Father that much more approachable.

Holy Spirit

Allusive one, hardest to describe, yet ever present and never ending; the eye-opener to the Truth. I began to understand You better when You first introduced me to Your infilling; to MY infilling, actually. You were that bursting water balloon, exploding within and running out from the core of my being into every square inch of my personhood. You are forever standing at the front of the classroom and speaking, as any good teacher would do, on what it is I need to know to get me to that next level of study.

Then You take me out into the field and make me experience the lesson.

You throw me into the deep end of the pool and leave the swimmies on the deck chair. You push me out of the airplane, reminding me at the same time where the zipper to my chute is located. You test me without warning, pull a surprise quiz and let me take the test over and over again until I pass.

You're not mad about those dozens of times I fail.

You're the one I go to when the lights go out and the batteries have died and all the energy has drained from my body. You are where the engine gets its steam, the outlet gets its electricity, the generator gets its gasoline. You help me speak, help me remember, help me discern, help me period.

You were always there. With the Father, with the Son, and now with me.

"God in three persons, blessed Trinity."

Bits And Pieces

I have discovered that most people will read something that is short and sweet and will not be drawn to something that is long and dragged out. Sesame Street uses this same concept when it puts a half hour of instruction together in 3 to 4 minute spurts. Children can't handle more than that.

Now it applies to adults as well. We are in such a hurry and we want you to get on with it and make your point. Count the number of seconds in TV and online commercials today. Point made.

And we love story-telling. Sometimes, it's the best part of a sermon. It's the part we remember. It's the part we can identify with. It's the part that puts the punch to the point being made.

That I write in vignette style is God's happy design. That I have so many stories I want to tell you is God's happy plan. That I have not been happy on this journey is God's happy intention. It has led me to seeing that He is the golden thread that weaves all these adventures together. The stories **are** the sermons.

Isn't that exactly what Jesus did? He told stories, to make a point, and the Holy Spirit, if we are really listening, is telling the story behind the story. Our job is to listen for that voice of Truth. That's the punch I'm talking about. That's the one I get hit with all the time. That's a punch that has no abusive intention behind it.

For Crying Out Loud

I was told by one of my college professors, in the 1960's, that my writing was bold and brash and more along the lines of how someone would *think* and not necessarily *say* or *speak*. I wasn't at all sure if that was a compliment, but I took it as such and continued to write in that vein. I am now convinced, decades later, that it is a kind of gift woven into who I am and what I do. The softening of my unique style, which can fall into that brash category if left on its own, is Who God is in it and His wisdom is there to show me what to do with those thoughts.

Often what stirs in my mind is best left unsaid. Ditto that concept for the rest of the world, but that shouldn't be my excuse for messing up from time to time.

I was once shown something by the Lord that had three unique features: it was prophetic, it was true, and it should have been put in my Ponder Pocket and brought out at another time. I brought it out right away, told all the wrong people, and it came back to haunt me for a decade.

Right after that incident, I identified immediately with the Old Testament Joseph and his 16-year-old pubescent mouth. He mouthed off about something the Lord showed him and it backfired in his face. Of course it was not the first time I had blurted something out like that. It has taken years for me to learn this simple fact: God is all about truth as much as He's all about timing. He is the Way, the Truth, and the Life; He is also the Alpha and the Omega.

That said, I didn't tell any of these stories in order to stir up wrath or to have my words used to bait a bitching session. It's not my intention at all to supply anyone with another good reason to continue bad-mouthing pastors and Christians, even if they might be dead-wrong; even if what they did provided a "legitimate" reason to leave the church. I really don't want my readers getting angrier at the system than they might be already. And for those who are familiar with anyone mentioned in my stories, my intention is not to make them look bad. (Rom. 14:4 NRSV *Who are you to judge another's servant? To his own master he stands or falls. Indeed, he will be made to stand, for God is able to make him stand.*)

The reason I have told my story, I finally and clearly recognize, is because there are so many people who have wounds inflicted on them by the church and they can't get past the pain.

I think of the people I have encountered who have no desire to continue their walk with the Lord or to embrace any kind of relationship with His people ever again because of what was done to them by church leaders. I think of the angry Christians I have fellowshipped with for years who have lost complete faith in the gifts of the Spirit because they saw how the gifting and the gifts and the gifted were abused. I think of the multiple believers I have dined with who, after suffering a church hurt, prefer to stay at home and get their spiritual nourishment from Sunday morning television. I think of those who only refer to the Lord and church leaders using foul language and a fouler attitude.

I'm thinking of one woman I know who is so terribly scarred by her own marriage to a pastor—of course she is divorced—that to this day, she cannot even go into a church without vomiting.

I'm also thinking of a wounded sheep I recently met who continually uses the words "being raped" to describe her negative encounters with church leadership. While this seems to emulate out of her spewing, I find it interesting that she uses the same word that applied to the dream about how the elders in my church were dealing with me.

I'm going to take a broad leap here but I will take the leap nonetheless. I am going to consider three Scriptures—one I just used and two others—that are imperative to note in thinking about all the different people I have mentioned here and also to consider my boldness in my use of the word "rape." The passages are:

Rom.14:4 *"Who are you to pass judgment on servants of another? It is before their own lord that they stand or fall. And they will be upheld, for the Lord is able to make them stand."*

I Chron. 16:22 *"Do not touch My anointed ones and do My prophets no harm."*

I Samuel 26:11 *"The Lord forbid that I should stretch out my hand against the Lord's anointed."*

I'm going to ask you to consider turning this admonition in another direction completely. Consider the possibility that the one that was violated, the *victim,* is the 'anointed one.' Consider the possibility that it is the *elders* who are the ones passing judgment, who are not to do the touching.

This is exactly the same way the religious people looked upon Jesus as He walked the earth. We have the Bible stories and the hindsight to remind us, but did we lose the deeper meaning so quickly?

I asked a Christian male friend if he thought my use of the word *rape* was inappropriate and here is his reply:

"I think rape is very appropriate—physical rape can only hurt the body and soul. The kind of abuse—(spiritual) rape—that a spiritual leader and/or a church can do affects the spirit also—a much deeper wound. Physical can/does alienate the victim from men (often) and leads to (a) much lower trust level—how much worse when that alienation/distrust is transferred to the ultimate Man..."

"He who has an ear, let him hear what the Spirit says to the churches" (Rev. 3:22).

I have told my story from my viewpoint alone—from my peephole in the fence.

What the Lord did with me in my experience, and through it, is all I know. So while I wandered those hills and tripped over all those bruised, battered, and violated sheep, I came to the conclusion that damaged sheep are not healthy sheep and need to get well. I include myself among the damaged and have struggled through the healing process. I see where it is easy to walk away, to continue to slam and assault the offenders, where the television and I could be delightfully compatible. But it was Jesus Himself who posed the question: "Do you want to get well?" And, honestly, Who else can we truly go to in order to *get* well? I'm here to say that man messes up but Jesus cleans up messes. It's totally what He's all about. I chose to be healed and we are not done yet, Jesus and I.

Have the events of the last several years broken me?

Absolutely.

Have they allowed me the space and place to become a
    better person?

Absolutely.

Have I arrived?

Absolutely not.

Have I been reconciled with those who walked out of my
    life?

Not in the least. Even though some of us may talk to each other and express niceties, nothing comes remotely close to the closeness we once had so many years ago.

Do I miss that?

Absolutely.

Do I believe we can be fully reconciled?

Absolutely, but not necessarily in this lifetime.

Writing about what happened to me has been anything but cathartic. Reliving these stories by writing about them brought back many of the previous and rather horrific thoughts and feelings, and carried them back into my soul in full force. What is keeping me in a healthy place, while allowing me to move forward, is to constantly balance that resurrected pain with His Resurrection Promises. It is also far more important for the message to get out than for me to reach a kind of spiritual Utopia before I write.

My message? It is possible to love Jesus again and it is possible to trust His children again and someday we may actually attach the title of "pastor" in front of someone's first name and not wince.

For some reason, that pastor thing is the one thing I haven't been able to do just yet.

(wince)

Cover Story

Let me tell you about my artist friend who did the artwork on the cover of this book. You have to know something about her. She and her husband left my old church 20 some years ago because of the control thing. We rarely saw them after that, although she is originally from that area. Between eight and nine years ago the Lord told her something was happening in my home and to pray for me and my husband. She called a couple of weeks later to see what was up and we figured out that the day the Lord told her to pray was exactly the day I called 911!!!! She has been encouraging me in the Lord ever since.

I keep staring at the book cover she created and I see how fragile and transparent and broken the woman's figure is, and it suddenly hits me that when I started the book, I had no ending for it. I only knew to start writing it and the Lord told me I would know the purpose and the ending when I got there.

So when I got there—and it just so happened to be on Good Friday—I realized how change cannot happen without discomfort (or sheer agony, maybe) and my own brokenness is what allowed me to take in just a fraction of the power the Cross brings me.

It is a fact—I will always be breaking, I will always be "disjointed," to a degree. Jesus' body was never really physically broken as far as His bones were concerned, but it became terribly disjointed as it hung there on that Cross. Maybe that is exactly what is happening to His body even now—it is still one body but it is terribly disjointed.

So now I see it—the very people in the Kingdom who have been hurt and wounded are the very ones this book is written for. I'm not sure, even now, that I fully understand why I have gone through all this, but I am amazed that I have survived it. And if I have survived it, others can also "live to tell the story." Many of my new friends have been angry at the people who hurt me and they have defended me in much the same way as those who loved Jesus were mad at Pilate and mad at the crowd who said, "Crucify Him."

But there was a higher purpose—there is always a higher purpose—and I see it more clearly as the reality of what I say intensifies and the purpose of my writings begin to take shape in my own heart and bring change to my very character.

While I was working on this book, I had a prophetic word at my Tuesday meeting that was profound! The point of the prophecy was that these "beatings" I've endured on so many levels in the past were meant to bring me to the Lord and that there would be such a transformation that people wouldn't recognize the new ME. The woman who spoke it has known me since before I was a Christian. I am really not the person I was in 1973, yes, but I am also not the woman I was in 2003. Not close at all...

And here's the funny thing, the irony behind all that has transpired. I am becoming the very person the church leaders and my husband and family were looking for, on so many levels, and I actually believe they might like me this way...minus the brashness and boldness, maybe. (I was always told this was a negative trait and now am seeing it as a part of who I am. Okay,

so minus a little bit of flesh. ☺ I'm still working out how to balance it.)

I don't believe I am easily recognizable to the people of the past, and it has nothing to do with coloring my hair red. It has everything to do, however, with transformation. I am changing on the inside and the outside. My characteristics—even the ones that drove the religious community up the sacrilegious wall— are definitely changing and/or rearranging. I choose to let the changes happen because I choose to continue knowing this God I love.

My transformation is not finished, though. Of course it's not. You've read me between the lines and it's evident I'm still growing.

These things take time, like realizing just what the Lord's love for us is all about. I cannot even fathom the whole concept of the Cross, but I will take its purpose into my heart one step at a time. For those of you still feeling the sting of your hurt and rejection—our only healing balm is found in the love of Christ. We must ask Him to pour it into us, but only in "squirts." I don't think we could handle one lump sum; it would flatten us out.

In spite of the disjointing, both the figure on the book cover and myself are exactly where we all should be—void of the strings that once restricted us and kneeling before the Cross, trusting that the One who went there has indeed finished the work, just as He said. He is waiting for us to recognize both Him and the finished work and there is a road we need to travel to get there. Healing happens in the journey.

All our junk has no other choice but to leave, but only as we continue to set our minds and wills to believe in one very simple truth:

We are fully loved by the Creator of the Universe, and there's nothing we can do to prevent it, earn it, or deserve it. That is called grace.

An Attitude Of Gratitude

I am filled with gratitude to the Lord for sticking it out with me and for sending me all the body parts I was missing. He sent me friends who understood and cared and old friends from the past who wanted to resurrect our relationship. He sent me faithful and fabulous girlfriends, women who might not have a specific chapter written about them but contributed greatly to this chapter of my life. They know who they are.

Some were sent to me for just one season and just one reason and are gone. But they are not forgotten and are certainly appreciated.

Most of these people I never met until after the bus crash.

One of those "Body parts" shared a famous quote with me from Dr. Hans Rookmaaker: *"Jesus didn't come to make us Christian. Jesus came to make us fully human."*

The whole of these body parts have shown me a lot about what Jesus is probably like. And now He's teaching me to zero in on looking for Him within each one of them.

" Do unto others as you would want them to do unto you."

We are connected, after all!

Scars

Many times Christians say to an emotionally suffering brother or sister in Christ: "This too shall pass."

I am not fond of that phrase and its implications that everything will be done and over once you get past the hurting part. I do believe a person can get past the pain but I don't believe, if we are to be "fully human," that in time it will be as if it never was. It is through difficulty and depression and great hurt that we can allow the Lord to transform us as we walk through it and bear it, but it never truly passes and is gone. It leaves its mark and it might be called a scar. Scars, in any form, are permanent reminders. They do NOT pass. Whatever the "this" is that we think passes, only changes shape. Hopefully it is in the shape of healing—from appearing ugly to becoming a beautiful reminder that we have survived and we are healthier. As I mentioned earlier, scars should show others where we came from, but should not be the basis for where we are going.

Unwrapping the Wounded

One of the people who has played a huge part in my healing is the leader of the-living-room-pack that meets on Tuesday morning. She wrote this vignette and shared it with me. So while I'm stealing her words, she has requested anonymity. We know who she is.

It was obvious that Lazarus had received a miracle of "resurrected life" when he responded to Jesus' words, "Come out!" Either he walked out on his own or was somehow jet-propelled to the entrance of the cave where he had lain dead for four days. And, while it might have been much easier to use a pair of surgical shears or bush trimmers to cut through the layers of damp, dirty, stinkin', linen embalming strips, Jesus turned to the people at the gravesite and said, "(YOU) take off the grave clothes and let him go...."

HUH? Why didn't Jesus finish the job He started ... why did He involve the crowd in unwrapping Lazarus?

It is Jesus Who calls us out of darkness into His marvelous light, and the Holy Spirit Whose energy enables us to do so. "BUT," He says to the Body of Christ, "I have a job for you to do ... I'm calling you to help take off the grave clothes and assist this *new life* to understand that YOU care, by taking part in

309

the restoration, nurturing and caring of this one that I love!!"

So .... where is the obvious place to start the *unwrapping* process? Let's start with the **head**, for the mind is in need of being renewed.... The old paradigms, mindsets, thought processes and "stinkin' thinkin" associated with the *old man* have to go!! Renewal of the mind takes discipline and often (most usually) some accountability.... This is NOT an overnight process! The spiritual **eyes,** now opened to a new way of looking at things (and people), struggle to focus through a different set of lenses. Next, the **ears,** another discipline of *tuning out* the hurtful language of the past, and learning to tune in to the voice of the Holy Spirit Who reminds you that you are now loved, not rejected, not a failure, but competent. Next the **tongue ...** ooh, a "biggie," with its "natural" ability to criticize, gossip, slander, and rehearse the hurtful events of the past now finds new expression of thanksgiving, rejoicing, and praise! And as a covering over all this, we've been given the Helmet of Salvation.

I guess the **neck** comes next, allowing the head to turn more freely, and lending more than a narrow and limited view (especially ... and hopefully) of the Body of Christ!

As the unwrapping continues, the **heart** is no longer bound by tradition, ritual, "religious" entrapments, etc., but is finally free to beat in

310

rhythm with the heart of the Father! Sometimes a pacemaker, in the form of a close friend or accountability group, helps in assuring that the heart does not stop beating, while the Breastplate of Righteousness covers this vital organ!

As the **arms** are released, they lose their stiffness and eventually find a natural ability to be raised in praise and thanksgiving for newfound freedom! And the fingers, once used for pointing to the wrongs and hurtful personalities once encountered, are now clutching the Sword of the Spirit and the Shield of Faith, engaging in protection of self and others!

Continuing to take off the grave clothes, we finally come to the **feet,** which once walked in "religious shoes," now fitted with new "running shoes" to *run the race* with a clear goal in sight and the ability to jump and praise God along the way!

Yes, the Body of Christ has been given an awesome, and rewarding assignment to "unwind and loose" those who have been bound in religious grave clothes, by loving, accepting, and encouraging them to a new AND abundant life in Christ!

This unwrapping is exactly what the Lord and so many of my spiritual sisters (and a few such brothers) have so graciously done for me. My desire is that others wrapped up in death cloths would allow healers to help loosen their bonds. There truly are heart-healers out there, people you can trust to help you heal, people who will not cause you harm.

The Hearing Box

I have a rectangle box that I keep near me every day, right by my feet and just under my desk. It is the kind of box you might find a pair of shoes in, a box I like to call my Hearing Box. It has bronze handles on both sides of it, and the corners of the top are reinforced with bronze edging. There are pictures of various vessels all around the box and on its top. Each one of the vessels, from urns to pitchers to glass globes, is carrying various species of flowers. The dominant colors are yellow and gold tones and something was done to the look of the paper to give it that old, antique finish appearance. It is the kind of thing my eyes like to rest on. And they do.

Inside I keep my treasures. They are the physical, tangible proofs or symbols that remind me I have heard from the Lord. Amongst them are the slightly deflated I love you balloon, the broken Precious Moments statue, the note that came with the two dozen red roses that awful Valentine's Day and, well, other treasures bearing pleasant memories; little, intimate things for only me and the Lord to know about.

The box is my own personal altar of remembrance, my mountain of stones.

Most especially, it reminds me that I hear, and hear clearly, the echo of His voice as it travels to this side of heaven, flows into my ear holes, and lands straight in my heart.

Be-Ginning Again

We're all familiar with the phrase: We are not human doings, we are human beings. "Being" is the Word-of-the-Day here. To BE in Christ is an imperative truth for us to grasp. We have to fight the kind of thinking that tells us we are to do something more for God in order to be in right standing with Him. I call it the Santa Claus syndrome—trying to get on his "nice" list. It's so easy to fall into that way of thinking, to add to law, and we have a Congress that works overtime to remind us of how easy it is to keep adding and adding to the list of "do not's." (Oops! I said I'd only talk about the government one time. Sorry.)

The doing is done, and it happened at the Cross. Wrapping our heads around that one truth is our job for our lifetime. What we do for the Lord after accepting that fact becomes the fulfillment of the law itself, without walls and without restriction. We're given access, and the divine right, to explore the width and depth and breadth of what I can only call being human. In light of the One we are coming to know, we see ourselves more clearly and with that clarity, learn the art of surrendering to the transformation process of becoming more divine.

In Christ alone.

My greatest fear about submitting to a legalistic system is that the magnitude of this transformation process is diminished, especially when we entrust our perceptions and understandings of who God really is to an appointed leader. We must learn that listening to great teachings needs to be in addition to, not a replacement of, our personal time at His feet. Otherwise, we lose the ability, no, the gift, of discovering Him on our own.

Follow The Leader

That is the real poison in legalistic thinking—to develop a real or perceived dependency on leadership to do for you what it is you're supposed to be doing with the Lord directly. It is, I am convinced, born out of a need for acceptance and belonging and has made all of us who are already broken, that much more vulnerable and gullible. Unfortunately, we often put ourselves in the wrong pair of hands. We are looking for father-figures or spouses or best friends or brothers and sisters, and none of this is wrong in itself. We can find these people in the Body of Christ; they exist for our joy and our pleasure. They are gifts from God to help us through life and encourage us in our walk with the Lord. But they are not there to *replace* the Lord.

The job of the pastor and his leadership team is exactly the same as the other members of the Church—to be our cheering section; to catch us when we fall and lift us back up again; to labor in prayer for us; and to gently and lovingly say a liberating, revealing word from the Lord to show us where we have veered off the path or have unconsciously become the frog in the pot, like my lady in the kitchen did for me. We are all priests and kings.

The damage occurs when those in leadership are moved into a place reserved for God alone. It's so easy for us to let that happen and one reason for this is basically simple: the process of knowing God is hard work.

Having a relationship with any one person is hard work. But having it with the Creator of the universe is back-breaking, armpit sweating, brow-beating work. Jesus is not Mr. Rogers in a robe. He is not a helpless baby in a feeding trough. He is complicated, demanding, consuming, and always, always right.

I am becoming undone with knowing that and knowing Him.

Trying to explain anything about Jesus making entrance into your heart and your life and your thinking is an insurmountable task. To quote Walter Wink: "If Jesus had never lived, we would not have been able to invent him." *

In fact, the religious concept of the God/man who is Jesus is a little bit different from what the legalists were both suggesting and demonstrating. He is far more complicated and a lot less critical.

In truth, I can't seem to get away from the man. He allowed every rug to be pulled out from under me, so I could find Him in a new way. He's truly the Hound of Heaven, able to sniff me out no matter where my feet or my mind take me. I can't shake Him and I really don't want to. After all, I'm the one who said I wanted a man to love me unconditionally and He said, "Here **I am.**" At least He hates divorce and won't file the papers. He remains with me, faithful and steady. He won't reject me when I mess up or I walk away or I decide not to talk to Him for a few days while I reset my gears. He can handle excessive drama, pouting, and pity parties.

There is something so supernatural about this love from above that keeps me crawling back to His feet over and over again. Each time, I hand Him my heart, again. Each time, I am aware of His approval of me again and that one thing alone becomes the constant in my life. It becomes the basis that transforms me into becoming the woman He created me to be.

And, thank God, He is allowing me to be totally myself. I missed me all those years—the me that I lost from being spiritually "raped."

I am learning to understand in my heart that He loves me intensely. Knowing Him has become the most complex, fulfilling relationship I have ever tackled. And while it has not been easy, nor a pleasure cruise, it is always me who makes it hard and it is always me who gets us lost.

When, in the past, I let other people be a substitute for Him in my life, the relationships ended. They ended up one-sided, they ended up becoming a performance routine, and they ended up leaving bruises.

Biblical history shows us that God Himself did all He could to keep us from appointing a leader. He knows our vulnerability. He knows our apathy. He knows our bent toward laziness. And He knows that same vulnerability, apathy, and laziness that exist in whoever it is we appoint to that position of leader.

More importantly, He knows the outcome is not only our loss, but His as well. He loses a part of our heart that should be, rightfully, His. Others just don't know its contents like the Lord.

Engaging the Powers: Discernment and Resistance in a World of Domination by Walter Wink, Minneapolis: Fortress Press 1992, p. 136.

A Song

Following is a song that needs sharing, one that sprang forth from the heart of a dear sister who was also "excommunicated and disfellowshipped" and is learning, like me, there is only one place to turn for healing and it isn't inward.

You're Mine

I was abused, let down and used.

I was betrayed, called a renegade, I was accused.

And I was crying, cause they were lying—and believing
them had cost me.

So I prayed and I prayed.

And I kept down on my knees—until I heard Him say:

"I'll never leave you, I'll never forsake you.

I'll never leave you, I'll never forsake you.

Child, child, child, you're a child of mine.

You've endured the test of time—and you're mine."

I came unglued with deadly wounds.

Tried to forgive—just to live—but I was ruined.

And I was dying—resentment flying.

I knew I had to let it go.

So I prayed every day.

And I kept down on my knees—until I heard Him say:

"I'll never leave you, I'll never forsake you.

I'll never leave you, I'll never forsake you.

Child, child, child. You're a child of mine...You're Mine!"

Written by Jennifer Payne

Not Guilty Anymore

Written by Aaron Keyes

It doesn't matter what you've done.
It doesn't matter where you're coming from.
It doesn't matter where you've been.
Hear Me tell you I forgive.

You're not guilty anymore. You're not filthy anymore.
I love you. Mercy is yours.
You're not broken anymore. You're not captive anymore.
I love you. Mercy is yours.

Can you believe that this is true?
Grace abundant I am giving you.
Cleansing deeper than you know.
All was paid for long ago.

You're not guilty anymore. You're not filthy anymore.
I love you. Mercy is yours.
You're not broken anymore. You're not captive anymore.
I love you. Mercy is yours.

There is now therefore no condemnation
For those who are in Jesus.

You're not guilty anymore. You're not filthy anymore.
I love you. Mercy is yours.
You're not broken anymore. You're not captive anymore.
I love you. Mercy is yours.

You are spotless.
You are holy.
You are faultless.
You are whole.
You are righteous.
You are blameless.
You are pardoned.
You are Mine.

You're not guilty anymore. You're not filthy anymore.
I love you. Mercy is yours.
You're not broken anymore. You're not captive anymore.
I love you. Mercy is yours. Mercy is yours. Mercy is yours.

Love Squared

The love and grace of God astound me. I am so grateful that He has been pursuing me all these years and has refused to let up. While I have struggled to get to know Him and what He is all about, I found myself using the phrase, "out of the box" a lot. It had nothing to do with my box of remembrance but an entirely different one. It contains only His love and He keeps it at His own feet. I guess you could say it is His footstool.

This commitment, this covenant, this great affection He has for His creation is set within the framework of a sort of existential box and does not exist outside those pre-set perimeters. He has made promises to us, promises that cannot be broken or deviated from because He Himself has chosen to stay within the confines of His word, His oath, His covenant of love. In a sense, He has allowed Himself to stay within a box of His own choosing. He has formed His own definition of love and given Himself restrictions about what that love will and will not do. Perhaps in the light of eternity do the sides, at least figuratively, appear to vanish. But until then it is held securely in His Promise to keep His own professed Word.

While God Himself has set His own limitations, our human understanding of that kind of love will never grasp any of it until it is transferred into our own hearts. We will never truly fathom the whole of it till we reach eternity. So while we receive it by faith, it is evidenced by transformation. It is not God who changes, but us. Ironically, His love pushes out whatever growth-stunting restrictions and bondages that have trapped us and allows us to break out into His spacious box of love and become what we were called to be.

Once again, as on the Cross, He allows Himself to be tied down that we can be set free.

To believe this is true and to fully comprehend it, allows the ugly walls that box me in to begin to crumble. Like a chrysalis breaking down around me, the person I was created to be can emerge; the caterpillar can become the butterfly.

While I was writing this book, I heard the Lord say Bruised Reed, and I thought it was supposed to be the title of this book. But, it turned out He was giving me the promise—*A bruised reed He will not break.** While separating my stories—break in, out, down, through, and away—it was a promise to me that in all of these breakings, I myself will not break—I will survive this. This was and is incredibly good news. It has been such a struggle to get through these last several years—uphill with a backpack filled with bricks.

If you are still limping from the injuries inflicted on you in your own bus crash, allow the Holy Spirit to triage your wounds. He is the only One who Knows just how deeply your internal injuries have settled, even if you think you've hidden the fact that something inside still hurts.

May you emerge from your own brokenness and allow the Lord to begin the healing process. May you find Him to be far more gracious, incredibly kind, and insanely more loving than you could ever imagine.

Haven't you, really, been missing Him?

Haven't you, honestly, been missing you?

May you find yourself again, only this time, fully in Him. He's waiting. He's always been waiting.

* Isaiah 42:3 and Matthew 12:20

Shredded

I was about six years old, give or take a year, and the fact that I remember the incident so clearly is evidence that the mind seems only to recall more clearly the times of terror rather than the times of joy. It wasn't all that horrific, when I view it at my age and with all that space of time in the middle—six full decades later. But still when it comes to light, it makes me cringe!

I think it encompasses everything I have said in this book in one little story.

My dad always had problems with his teeth. They were extremely sensitive and he had difficulty chewing foods that had any degree of firmness to them. It was especially true of his favorite cereal—Shredded Wheat. While he loved the taste of it, he abhorred the texture. He would soak the large rectangle-shaped biscuits under water first, to soften the texture, and then do the milk and sugar thing.

Which is why, the morning I got up earlier than either of my parents, I decided to make my father his breakfast, just as he liked it. It required doing something I was forbidden to do—climb up on the sink. There was no other way for me to reach the faucet so I could soak the cereal first. I used a chair to get to the sink and sitting on the counter, I held the two pieces under the running water and massaged them to work in the softness I knew he liked.

It was all about pleasing Daddy.

That's when he walked into the kitchen and saw me. That's when I got the very first really bad beating I can remember vividly. Dad never saw what it was I was doing for him but rather what it was I should not be doing.

And somewhere in my memory of that incident, I hear my own voice, penetrating the loud sobs and saying, "But I wetted it, Daddy, I wetted it like you wanted."

The struggle has been in facing the old memories and the old belief systems and the old responses and replacing the lies in them with the truth. The truth is simply that I am loved by the Creator of the Universe. He lives in my heart and I live in His. He looks on me and He sees His Son and He is pleased. He sees me sitting on the counter near the sink and soaking the cereal. He watches my little face turning to His as I grin at Him and tell Him I wetted it, too, just the way He likes it.

And He grins back. He is well pleased.

Timeline of My Life

1947	Born
Early 1950s	Parents first break-up and problems with my uncle
Early 1960s	Priest problems
1963	Parents' marriage annulled
1964	Graduated high school
1965-1973	In and out of college and odd jobs
April 22, 1973	Born again
May 1973	Graduated college
1974	Soon-to-be husband ordained
June 1975	Married
1979	Miscarried
1984	Adopted our daughter
1988 or 89	Dad's apology to me
1991	Dad died. Also my uncle died that same year.
Spring 2002	Trouble discovered in the foundation of our house
Spring 2002	Starting to have visible, emotional problems from the oppression of being under legalism
Summer 2002	Began putting Scripture verses all over my house
May 16, 2003	The Awakening
2003	Started attending the Tuesday morning group
2003	Met Grace
October 2003	Moved into "divided" house
2004	Forced retirement
December 2004	Called 911
2005	Met Joy and began listening to Graham Cooke

2005	Called people to tell them I forgive them
2005	Joy paid for a year of Christian counseling for me.
April 2005	"I love you" balloon came to my house
December 2005	My step mom died
Valentine 2006	No-Mantic meal
2006	Began renting out a room in my house
August 2006	Divorce final
2006	Met Sharon
2006	Got paid for trees having to be cut down in my yard
August '06-May '07	Bible College
Summer 2007	Was taken to a mental hospital
2007	Found the blue robe
Valentine 2008	Received roses
August 2008	Started Graduate School with a scholarship
2009	Grad school discovered another scholarship
May 2010	Graduated with MA degree
2010	Started writing this book
2011	Moved out of the area
2011	Saved from bad deal when people bought my house with cash
2005-2011	Church-Hopped
Fall 2011	Began attending my home church

Putting this timeline together was a struggle for me because when you're going through trauma, you are unaware of time. It's hard to describe, but I've talked to other people who've experienced trauma and they say the same thing.

Broken

a pastor's wife shares her story

is available at:

olivepresspublisher.com

amazon.com

barnesandnoble.com

and other websites.

The E-book is available at:

amazon.com

Book stores and book distributors
may obtain this book through:

Ingram Book Company
or by e-mailing

olivepressbooks@gmail.com

To schedule the author

Carol DuPré

as a speaker,

contact her at:

caroldopray@yahoo.com

CPSIA information can be obtained at www.ICGtesting.com
Printed in the USA
BVOW01s0823250913

331587BV00008B/8/P